50 GREAT INDIANS

Rachna Chhabria is a children's author, columnist, blogger and a freelance journalist. As a child, she loved listening to stories, and now she loves writing them. Fantasy is one of her favourite genres.

She is the author of *Chaos in the Jungle and Other Stories* (2022), *Festival Stories through the Year* (2018), *Lazy Worm Goes on a Journey* (2014), *The Lion Who Wanted to Sing and Other Stories* (2006) and *Bunny in Search of a Name and Other Stories* (2006). Her stories have appeared in Young World, Open Sesame, *Tele Kids* and *Deccan Herald* student edition, several anthologies and school textbooks. She also writes columns for *Deccan Chronicle* and *The Asian Age*.

50 GREAT INDIANS

Extraordinary Lives, Inspiring Tales

RACHNA CHHABRIA

Published by
Rupa Publications India Pvt. Ltd 2022
161-B/4, Gulmohar House,
Yusuf Sarai Community Centre,
New Delhi 110049

Sales centres:
Bengaluru Chennai
Hyderabad Kolkata Mumbai

Copyright © Rachna Chhabria 2022

The views and opinions expressed in this book are the author's own and the facts are as reported by her which have been verified to the extent possible, and the publishers are not in any way liable for the same.

All rights reserved.
No part of this publication may be reproduced, transmitted, or stored in a retrieval system, in any form or by any means, electronic, mechanical, photocopying, recording or otherwise, without the prior permission of the publisher.

P-ISBN: 978-93-5520-440-0
E-ISBN: 978-93-5520-441-7

Fifth impression 2025

10 9 8 7 6 5

The moral right of the author has been asserted.

Printed in India

This book is sold subject to the condition that it shall not, by way of trade or otherwise, be lent, resold, hired out, or otherwise circulated, without the publisher's prior consent, in any form of binding or cover other than that in which it is published.

For my brother Deepak Chhabria,
who sets new benchmarks of perfection every single day

Contents

Introduction   xi

1. Ajay Thakur: In a Tough Situation, Be Brave and Fight Back   1
2. Amitabh Bachchan: Use Criticism to Your Advantage   5
3. A.P.J. Abdul Kalam: Walk on the Path of Righteousness   9
4. A.R. Rahman: Adopt an Experimental Approach   13
5. Bachendri Pal: Nudge Your Fear Aside   17
6. Bhimsen Joshi: Challenge Yourself   21
7. Bhupen Hazarika: Set a Trend   25
8. Birju Maharaj: Pursue Your Passion with Your Heart and Soul   29
9. Devi Shetty: Think Out of the Box   33
10. Dhundiraj Phalke: Believe in Yourself   37
11. Dhyan Chand: Keep Your Passion Alive   41
12. Ela Bhatt: Make Self-Reliance a Way of Life   45
13. E. Sreedharan: Make Time Your Ally   49
14. Gulzar: Be Flexible   53
15. Hafeez Contractor: Build a Strong Team   57
16. Hariprasad Chaurasia: Where There Is a Will, There Is a Way   61
17. Homi Bhabha: Develop Your Foresight   65

18. Kailash Satyarthi: Let Your Inspiration Forge Your Path 69
19. Kalpana Chawla: Dream, Dream and Dream Some More 73
20. Kiran Mazumdar-Shaw: Manifest Your Inner Strength 77
21. Leander Paes: Age Is Just a Number 81
22. Leila Seth: Break the Glass Ceiling 85
23. Mahadevi Verma: Give a Free Rein to Your Creativity 89
24. Mahendra Singh Dhoni: Channel Your Inner Zen 93
25. Mata Amritanandamayi Devi: Be the Change You Want to See 97
26. Mithali Raj: Adapt to Your New Role 101
27. M.S. Subbulakshmi: Never Give Up on Your Dedication 105
28. M.S. Swaminathan: Align with a Vision 109
29. Nandalal Bose: Find Your Groove 113
30. N.R. Narayana Murthy: Treat Failure as a By-Product of Success 117
31. Pankaj Advani: Focus on the Moment 121
32. P.C. Sorcar: Believe in Magic 125
33. Rajinikanth: Find Your Own Unique Style 129
34. R.K. Laxman: Look for the Unusual in the Usual 133
35. R.K. Narayan: Find Inspiration Everywhere 137
36. Ramkinkar Baij: First Learn the Rules, Then Break Them 141
37. Ritu Kumar: Blend the Old with the New 145
38. Rukmini Devi Arundale: Be a Game Changer 149
39. Salim Ali: Retain Your Curiosity and Your Keenness to Learn 153

40. Sam Manekshaw: Have the Courage of Your Convictions	157
41. Shahnaz Husain: You Can Make Your Own Destiny	161
42. Shakuntala Devi: Discover Your Own Wonderland	165
43. Sunderlal Bahuguna: Take the Macro Perspective	169
44. Sunil Chhetri: Make Discipline a Lifestyle	173
45. Tarla Dalal: Keep It Simple	177
46. Verghese Kurien: Invoke the Perseverance Trait	181
47. Vikram Sarabhai: Take the Road Less Travelled	185
48. Vinoba Bhave: Stand up for What You Believe In	190
49. Y.K. Hamied: Sometimes Put Others before Yourself	194
50. Zubin Mehta: Keep Your Sense of Awe and Wonder Alive	198
Acknowledgements	202

Introduction

India is a land of greatness: great thinkers and scientists, great monuments and discoveries, great philosophers and saints, great food and festivals, great discoveries and people.

Greatness is both a virtue and a personality trait, but in the case of the personalities featured in this book, it's a habit. An intrinsic habit that made them take the road less travelled, that made them change the course of their destinies, made them the first to achieve certain goals in their fields and set new benchmarks and milestones.

50 Great Indians is a celebration of some of these Indians who have contributed to the greatness of this country in many ways.

Choosing just 50 people was an extremely difficult task, as India is a land of great people in all spheres of life, people who not just carved different paths but walked over it, time and again, guiding and leading thousands of Indians.

Success wasn't easy for them, neither was life smooth; they all had difficult choices to make, and obstacles blocked their paths at every turn. But one thing they all had in common was the determination and the sheer willpower that made them overcome the roadblocks confronting them frequently. Their goal was always clear. When they fell, they got up, dusted themselves and rejoined the race. It was their grit that made them turn the word 'impossible' to 'I will do it'.

These personalities: scientists, musicians, doctors, writers, spiritual leaders, sportspersons, cinema artists, dancers, industrialists—all of them have brought India under the global spotlight.

While researching for this book, I not just got to know these personalities a little better, but I also realized that each and every one of them has taught us many lessons. But for the purpose of this book, I had to focus on just one lesson. The lesson I chose was what not just defined the person, it was also the essence of their personality. These lessons are our inheritance, a legacy that will hold us in good stead in life.

From the teenage boy who changed his subject in college to one that would enable him to help farmers produce more crops, to the young boy who practised with a carrom board, matchbox and chopsticks so that he could excel at his chosen sport, they both were guided by a vision. From the young boy who sold newspapers to add to the family income, to the young girl who gave food and clothes from her house to the needy, both showed that they were following their heart, their actions guided by kindness and compassion. From the young girl who rolled newspapers and sang pretending that it was a mike to the girl staring curiously at the stars and planes, both followed their desire, giving wings to their dreams.

Along the path to the fulfilment of their dream, their life became a lesson for the next generation of Indians, and their achievements, a testimony of their faith and belief in their abilities and in themselves.

As a nation, it's time to relive their contributions through this book. My endeavour is to bring them back into the collective consciousness of a generation unfamiliar with their journey and struggles, unfamiliar with their achievements and deeds.

This book was a lesson in humility. I was, at turns, overwhelmed and awed by the great personalities, and what they all set out to achieve in life and what they all faced in their journey.

I fervently hope I have done some justice through my words to the immense achievements of these great Indians. I also hope that lessons from these masters will help us reach our goals and fulfil our dreams.

1

AJAY THAKUR

*In a Tough Situation,
Be Brave and Fight Back*

Not everyone can don the cape of bravery. Though light, the cape is heavy for the wearer, thus weighing them down. Most people give in to despair when faced with a tough situation, but there are always some who demonstrate their bravery by fighting the circumstances.

When a girl is being teased on the road, most people walk past quietly, pretending they haven't noticed anything; in contrast, sometimes, a lone figure stands up to the eve-teasers, unmindful of the consequences. Faced with a tough situation, the person chose to be brave and fought back, becoming the voice of strength.

In a train, when a woman's handbag is being snatched by pickpockets, she doesn't allow the criminals to run away with her hard-earned money but choses to fight the assailants by channelling her bravery.

During recess in school when a boy is being bullied, while the other boys watch quietly, fearing retribution from the bully, a single figure stands up to the bully, telling a few home truths and showing the bully a mirror, reflecting their distorted image.

The boy standing up has chosen to be brave in a tough situation and has decided to fight back.

It is this quality of fighting back that we can see in Ajay Thakur, one of the best professional kabaddi players that India has seen, especially when he is dealing with a stressful situation on the field. The former captain of the Indian national kabaddi team is an attacking player, known to have snatched his team from the jaws of defeat several times. Every time his team fell into critical situations during a match, Thakur, the star raider of the team, turned the match around with his superb moves, earning himself the title of a 'match winner'.

Born on 1 May 1986 in Dabhota, a small village in the Solan district of Himachal Pradesh, Thakur had a regular childhood. Since his father, Chhotu Ram, was a national-level wrestler and also a coach, Thakur was exposed to sports from an early age. While his father trained him, it was his mother, Rajinder Kaur, a school teacher, who inspired a disciplined approach to both his career and life.

When Thakur was a young boy, one day he saw his uncle distributing laddoos in the village, as his cousin (his uncle's son), Rakesh Kumar Chandel, playing for the national team, had won a medal. This incident turned inspirational, sowing the seed in Thakur's mind that he too wanted to see his parents celebrate his victory by distributing laddoos in the village. With this goal set in his mind and life, Thakur started playing kabaddi with the boys in the village, honing his skills. Thakur was so fond of the game that once he even ran away from home to play in a kabaddi tournament.

Thakur began his career as a professional kabaddi player when he made his debut in the Indian team at the age of 19. He won his first international medal at the Asian Indoor Games in 2007.

Credited with inventing a new move called the Frog Jump,

Thakur's flying leaps helped India clinch many victories. The way he escapes the opposing team's clutches during a raid is creditworthy; he has fine-tuned the escape to an art that leaves the spectators gasping in awe and asking for more. When the Indian team is in a tough situation or trailing behind, very often it is Thakur who is sent to the opposing side. Thakur, the raid specialist, knows that he has no option but to be brave and fight back. At a strapping 6'1", Thakur has the advantage of reaching out for the midline even with the opponents tugging at him from all sides.

Thakur is an attacking player, and his quick-fire raids lasting 15 to 25 seconds are marked with a speed and an agility that leaves his opponents helpless, enabling him to win valuable points for his team, pushing them to the brink of victory. The trademark raids have several moves, from a toe touch to stunning back kicks, that take the opponents by surprise, and the lightning-quick hand touch while running back to his side has earned him the oppositions' respect as well as fear. It has also seen him piled with several monikers: 'Escape Artist', a testimony to his agility of escaping the clutches of his enemies' grip; 'Running Hand Touch Specialist', due to his lightning-quick touches; 'Flying Thakur', courtesy of the flying leaps he takes.

A player who keeps his calm throughout the game, Thakur was a part of the Indian kabaddi team defeating Iran in the 2014 Asian Games in Incheon, South Korea, to win the gold medal.

The 2016 Kabaddi World Cup saw Thakur at his stellar best. It was his career-defining moment. India had reached the finals and was pitted against Iran. With Iran taking a lead, India was trailing by 8 points. It was a do-or-die situation when Thakur snatched the game from the opponent's hands with his daring 4-point running raid and flying leap, giving India the lead, which his teammates capitalized on. India won the Kabaddi World Cup, and Thakur became the number-one raider for the tournament with maximum raid points. At 68 points, he was the highest scorer and was named the 'Man of the Tournament'.

In 2017, Thakur became the captain of the Indian side, leading his team to the gold at the 2017 Asian Kabaddi Championship in Gorgan, Iran, as well as the 2018 Kabaddi Masters tournament in Dubai, in which India defeated Iran 44–26 to win the match and the tournament, carving a niche for himself in the annals of the game with his stupendous performance.

Thakur, an Arjuna Award winner, has inspired many sportspersons to make their mark in kabaddi. He also has the honour of being the first male kabaddi player to be decorated with the Padma Shri in 2019, in the same year he married Sandeep Rana.

When not playing kabaddi, Thakur serves the country as a deputy superintendent of police (DSP) in the Himachal Pradesh Police. His motto 'When you encounter a tough situation, you have to be brave and fight back,' is instrumental in his success and also his philosophy of life.

2

AMITABH BACHCHAN

Use Criticism to Your Advantage

The thorns of criticism have seldom left anyone alone. Be it a child, an old man, a young woman or a teenager, criticism has trailed them like a faithful shadow. In school, we have all been told that our posture, whether standing in the assembly line or sitting in our chairs, is bad or that our handwriting isn't neat. At home, we are again at the receiving end of some kind of criticism masquerading as suggestions for our overall improvement. Professionals like teachers, doctors, engineers, writers and actors, all have constant criticism heaped at their doorstep. The easiest thing in life is to criticize others.

Animals, too, must have their fair share of criticism from other jungle creatures, who must think that the giraffe's neck is too long, the elephant's trunk too thick, the butterfly too light, and the ant, tiny. But these clever animals use these very traits that elicit criticism to their advantage. The giraffe uses its long neck smartly by devouring the tender leaves from the topmost branches of the trees, while the elephant utilizes its thick trunk to pluck and shove entire branches of bananas into its mouth. The feather-soft butterfly makes maximum use of its air-like lightness for perching on flowers and sucking its nectar, and the smart ant can find its way into the tiniest of spaces, foraging for food.

Very few people are able to shed the excess baggage of criticism; even fewer are able to use it to their advantage. Luckily for us, the superstar of Bollywood film industry, Amitabh Bachchan, made all the criticism piled against him work to his advantage.

Amitabh Harivansh Srivastava was born on 11 October 1942 in Allahabad (now Prayagraj) to Harivansh Rai and Teji Bachchan. He was initially named Inquilab, inspired by the phrase 'Inquilab Zindabad'. Later, he was renamed Amitabh (meaning, the light that will never die), and as his father, an established Hindi poet, had adopted the pen name Bachchan (meaning, childlike), Inquilab Srivastava came to be known as Amitabh Bachchan—a name now synonymous with brilliance. Growing up in a household dominated by poetry and theatre, a legacy of his parents, this interest in the performing arts rubbed off on Bachchan.

An alumnus of Sherwood College, Nainital, and Kirori Mal College, University of Delhi, Bachchan moved to Calcutta (now Kolkata) for his first job. Not content with a regular job, Bachchan realized that he wanted more from life. Quitting his job, Bachchan landed in Bombay (now Mumbai) in 1968, carrying his dreams in his heart. However, the ruthless city of dreams was anything but welcoming.

Bachchan's height (he is nearly 6'2"), his long legs, his tanned complexion and his deep baritone voice were rejected outright by the Hindi film industry, which with their penchant for fair complexion, shorter height and softer voices were taken aback by the unconventional personality of Bachchan. Though Bachchan faced many rejections, the fire of his dreams burnt bright and strong. Anyone else would have given up, but not Bachchan. His lucky break came in the form of *Saat Hindustani* (1969), a film in which he played one of the seven protagonists. Sadly, the film flopped, but Bachchan's role was noticed, earning him the National Film Award for Best Newcomer.

Initially, Bachchan managed to snag small roles, but his big break came in the form of Hrishikesh Mukherjee's *Anand* (1971), with Rajesh Khanna in the lead role. Bachchan's role of a cynical doctor won him his first Filmfare Best Supporting Actor award. But the film that set Bachchan on the path of superstardom was *Zanjeer* (1973). It was a film that had been rejected by several actors, as it went against the romantic and clean image they wanted to portray on screen. *Zanjeer* not only gave Bachchan the title of 'The Angry Young Man', it also gave wings to his career.

The entire nation fell in love with the traits that were the cause of Bachchan's initial rejection. Using all the criticism stacked against him, Bachchan aptly turned them in his favour by rolling out one hit after another in films such as *Sholay* (1975), *Deewaar* (1975), *Hera Pheri* (1976), *Don* (1978), *Trishul* (1978), *The Great Gambler* (1979), *Laawaris* (1981), *Kaalia* (1981), *Nastik* (1983) and *Agneepath* (1990), where he was the hero with shades of grey, channelling his inner angst and bitterness against society or against the establishment.

Bachchan's unconventional choice of roles played perfectly to his personality. He used his deep baritone to his advantage, mouthing dialogues that entered the popular lexicon. Film-watchers often repeated Bachchan's dialogue from *Kaalia*, '*Hum jahan khare ho jate hain, line wahin se shuru hoti hai*,' and it became a popular phrase for people trying to show their attitude. Another famous dialogue, '*Aaj khush to bahot hoge tum*,' from *Deewaar*, when Bachchan speaks to Lord Shiva inside a temple, is a scene often re-enacted by aspiring actors in their auditions. The way Bachchan said his name Vijay Deenanath Chauhan in the film *Agneepath*, adding '*baap ka naam Deenanath Chauhan, ma ka naam Suhasini Chauhan, gaon Mandva,*' made film buffs rewind their video players to listen to this line repeatedly.

Considered a one-man industry, Bachchan carried films on

his sturdy shoulders through the sheer brilliance of his acting and exceptional dialogue delivery, winning four National Film Awards as Best Actor, the Dadasaheb Phalke Award and 15 Filmfare Awards.

Credit for Bachchan's superstardom lies with his ability to constantly reinvent himself, which he did in films like *Baghban* (2003), *Black* (2005), *Sarkar* (2005), *Nishabd* (2007), *Cheeni Kum* (2007), *Sarkar Raj* (2008), *Satyagraha* (2013) and *102 Not Out* (2018), each role showcasing his versatility as an actor. Bachchan has come a long way, from the angry young man of *Deewaar* to the grumpy man with chronic constipation in *Piku* (2015); from playing a 13-year-old suffering from progeria in *Paa* (2009) to a man in love with a woman half his age in *Cheeni Kum*; from the retired lawyer representing three girls in the courtroom drama *Pink* (2016) to the lawyer in *Badla* (2019)—he has essayed all the roles with ease, slipping into the skin of his characters effortlessly. It's no wonder that he is on every director's wish list.

Felicitated with the Padma Shri, Padma Bhushan and the Padma Vibhushan for his contribution to the performing arts, Bachchan also received the Government of France's highest civilian honour—Officier de la Legion d'Honneur (Officer of the Legion of Honour).

Bachchan's success story has inspired hundreds of youngsters to board the train to Mumbai to pursue their celluloid aspirations. His is a truly remarkable story of struggle, perseverance, determination and hard work.

3

A.P.J. ABDUL KALAM

Walk on the Path of Righteousness

Though the term 'righteous' literally means always being right, especially in the context of morals, it's often associated with religion. But walking on the path of righteousness should come under the category of philosophy of life. It's the guiding principle steering one's life. Always doing the right thing, not just in connection with one's self or where one's welfare is concerned but with others too—that's what being righteous truly means.

The path of righteousness, though invisible to the rest of the world, is quite real and tactile, and clearly visible to the person walking on that path. For each person, this path is different. Lit as it is by the light of integrity, that path of righteousness also reveals the temptations in the form of detours and shortcuts that must be avoided.

The sense of righteousness is one of the most important attributes everyone should cultivate by making honesty one's personal policy for everything one does in life. Honesty not just defines a person but also creates the person's character.

Many of us must have heard this story in our childhood. To test the young students in his gurukul, a guru gave each student a banana, telling them that they must eat the fruit where no one can see them. A little later, all the students returned empty-handed, except one. Each student narrated where he had eaten the banana—someone had eaten it inside the stable, another in a corner of the cowshed, a third behind a tree and so on. Finally, it was the turn of the student who hadn't eaten the fruit given to him. His logic was that as God or the Creator is everywhere, seeing all his actions, there is no place he could have eaten it without anyone seeing him. This was the answer the guru wanted to hear.

Avul Pakir Jainulabdeen Abdul Kalam's entire life was a lesson in righteousness. The 11th President of India (in office from 2002 to 2007), Kalam earned the title People's President, a testimony to the immense popularity he enjoyed. An aerospace scientist, Kalam was known as the 'Missile Man of India' and played a major role in the development of India's missile and nuclear programmes.

Kalam was born on 15 October 1931 into a Tamil Muslim family in Rameswaram. His father, Jainulabdeen, was a boat-owner and also the imam of a local mosque, and his mother, Ashiamma, was a homemaker. At one time, Kalam's ancestors were wealthy, but over the years, the family's fortunes had dipped. Right from a young age, Kalam was keen on supporting his family financially. The youngest of four brothers and one sister, he sold newspapers at one time to add to the family income.

Kalam was a hard-working student, with a keenness for learning. After completing his schooling, he graduated in physics from St. Joseph's College, Tiruchirappalli, and went on to study aerospace engineering at the Madras Institute of Technology.

Kalam joined the Defence Research and Development Organisation (DRDO) as a scientist. This was the start of his long career in science. At DRDO, he designed a small hovercraft and, with a desire to accomplish more professionally, he also started working on an expandable rocket project.

A few years later, Kalam moved to the Indian Space Research

Organisation (ISRO), where he was the project director of India's first indigenously designed satellite launch vehicle—SLV-III, which successfully launched the Rohini satellite, RS-1, in near-earth orbit in July 1980.

After rejoining DRDO, Kalam was actively involved in India's civilian space programme and the development of ballistic missile and launch vehicle technology.

As the chief scientific adviser to the prime minister and secretary of the DRDO from July 1992 to December 1999, Kalam played an active role in the Pokhran-II nuclear tests conducted in 1998. As the chief project coordinator during the testing phase, Kalam came under the media limelight, gaining recognition as the country's best nuclear scientist and becoming a national hero.

Kalam was noted for his integrity and his simple lifestyle throughout his career. He had made the path of righteousness his personal path, never stepping out of its boundaries or even moving close to the edges. He was a man of spartan needs—his handful of personal possessions, his copy of a holy text, a few other books he held dear, his favourite veena, some clothes, a CD player and a laptop, could all be packed up in one suitcase. Even his food habits were frugal; a vegetarian, he enjoyed simple food. Kalam's morning routine included listening to devotional Carnatic music. He also enjoyed playing his veena, disappearing into its soothing music, and, in his free time, wrote Tamil poetry.

Once when Kalam was visiting Kentucky with his team, it was the month of April. The small trees there were blooming with flowers. Fascinated with the tree, Kalam inquired about it. His hosts told him that the tree was called dogwood. The tree's slender branches were used to make daggers, and over time, the tree's original name, dagwood, got distorted into dogwood. They further added that it was the state flower and unique to Kentucky. Kalam was displeased with the tree's name. Refusing to call the tree dogwood, he named it April Bloomer, even writing a poem on it. That's the path of righteousness Kalam followed, where even nature came under the umbrella of his concern.

There are many incidents highlighting Kalam's concerned nature and sense of propriety. While travelling with his team, Kalam would stay at Raj Bhavans in the state capitals. He would always insist on eating with his staff at the dining table. His logic was that if his staff ate separately, they wouldn't be given all the nice things he was served.

So strict was Kalam's path that it followed him in every sphere of life, influencing his thought process and emotions too. Once when Kalam was the subject of a comedian's jokes, he refused to take offence, saying that jokes were meant to be laughed at, not the subject of the jokes. His logic was that there was no need to feel offended, as tolerance to humour was an essential trait of a thinking, progressive society. He endorsed the view that all opinions must be accepted.

Always eager to be in the company of youngsters, Kalam launched a programme for the youth of India called the What Can I Give Movement in May 2012.

Kalam died on 27 July 2015 at the Indian Institute of Management in Shillong, when he collapsed after suffering a cardiac arrest while giving a lecture. The Bharat Ratna awardee has been truly described as a shining jewel in India's crown.

4

A.R. RAHMAN

Adopt an Experimental Approach

Mix-and-match style is a kind of experimental approach. Experimental not in the sense of the laboratory experiment but a casual one, where different items are combined to form a new and unique pattern or style. The mix-and-match style works for several objects: clothes, furniture, cuisine, upholstery, music and even food.

It is a favourite style of fashion designers: they like to blend different styles and cuts with various fabrics to create effects that are both innovative and path-breaking. Long brocade jackets with satin or silk saris, short tops with fitting pants, adding pleats to give it a twist, off-shoulder frilly blouses with sheer saris, polka-dot tops with striped bottoms, accompanied by accessories of different colours and so on.

This experimental approach is a bit risky because no one knows the overall effect of the entire outfit or the different accessories and clothes—whether it will clash or complement the outfit. For some brave souls, it's a style statement, giving them the opportunity to stamp their strong individuality on their chosen style; for others, it's a chance to blend different elements to create something new, something never tried before, which they themselves don't know the outcome of.

Just like fashion designers, some hairstylists, too, like to experiment by combining elements from different hairdos to create funky new ones. Making a Christmas-tree style hairdo complete with baubles or combining open hair with braids. And then there are make-up artists who embrace the bold, experimental approach, sometimes applying different shades of lipstick on the upper and lower lip.

By adopting an experimental approach in the true mix-and-match style, music composer A.R. Rahman has taken his career to the peaks of popularity and his music to new levels of genius, notching up chartbusters with regularity. Rahman's captivating and lilting tunes have driven his fans to ecstasy, making them hungry for more.

Born on 6 January 1967 in Madras (now Chennai), Rahman's birthname was A.S. Dileep Kumar. When he converted to Islam at the age of 23, he changed his name to Allah Rakha Rahman.

One of Rahman's earliest music influences was his father, R.K. Shekhar, a music composer and a music conductor for Tamil and Malayalam films. As a child, Rahman would often play the keyboard in his father's studio, thus discovering the melodious world of music. He also trained under the famous music teacher Master Dhanraj for some time in his childhood. His music teacher's proficiency in multiple instruments inspired Rahman, paving the way for his own expertise in various instruments.

Rahman's father passed away when he was barely nine years old, leaving his mother to assume the role of the breadwinner of the family. Rahman, too, chipped in to support his family, missing his classes in school and even his exams in the process. The family augmented their income by renting out the music equipment owned by Shekhar. When Rahman was 11, his father's friend M.K. Arjunan, noticing the boy's proficiency in music, offered him the opportunity to play in his orchestra.

After completing his schooling, first from Padma Seshadri Bala Bhavan and later from MCN School, Rahman joined the Madras Christian College Higher Secondary School based on his musical talent. There, he befriended several classmates, music aficionados like him, and together they formed a band, with Rahman playing the keyboard. Later, he formed a rock group called Nemesis Avenue. By now, Rahman had learned to play several instruments: piano, keyboard, harmonium, guitar and the synthesizer, acquiring a tremendous knowledge of each instrument and learning its advantages. Of all the instruments, Rahman was fascinated with the synthesizer, a perfect combination of music and technological advancement, and it had a huge impact on Rahman's music.

Armed with a diploma in western classical music, Rahman was ready to conquer the world with his tunes. Rahman's career started with him composing music for documentaries and jingles for advertisements.

Mani Ratnam's Tamil film *Roja* (1992), a love story with Kashmir as the backdrop, catapulted Rahman into instant stardom, winning him both commercial success and critical acclaim, and the coveted award for Best Music Director at the National Film Awards. Songs like '*Chinna Chinna Aasai*' set the ball rolling for Rahman's career.

Rahman's tunes graced many films: *Thiruda Thiruda* (1993), *Gentleman* (1993), *Kadhalan* (1994), *Bombay* (1995), *Indian* (1996), *Dil Se* (1998), *Jeans* (1998), *Taal* (1999), *Kandukondain Kandukondain* (2000), *Alaipayuthey* (2000), *Saathiya* (2002), *Swades* (2004), *Rang De Basanti* (2006), *Sivaji* (2007), *Ghajini* (2008), *Jodha Akbar* (2008) and *Rockstar* (2011), establishing his position as a hit composer. When Rahman started a recording studio in the backyard of his house, no one knew that the small studio would churn out chartbusters, becoming one of the most-advanced recording studios in Asia.

Rahman's music for *Rangeela* (1995) was both foot-tapping and unusual. *'Tanha Tanha'* with the flute music interspersed with stringed instruments, and the vibrancy of *'Rangeela Re'* remain unmatched. *'Kabhi Kabhi Aditi Zindagi'* from *Jaane Tu... Ya Jaane Na* (2008), with the guitar music blended with other musical instruments, will remain a favourite of many.

Rahman is not content with creating lilting soundtracks for films; the background scores he creates are haunting melodies, all its notes bearing the stamp of both his strong individuality as well as his experimental genius. Credit for his experimental approach can be laid at the doorstep of his training in western classical music, which often creeps into his background scores. His music is an amalgamation of traditional Indian instruments and contemporary instruments, and the result is a unique tune that constantly plays in the listener's mind.

These very attributes infuse Rahman's soundtracks with an unforgettable haunting quality that is timeless as well as fresh; every time one hears it, there is something new to discover in his music. Another innovation of Rahman is his usage of the harpejji. The stringed instrument, using the principles of guitar, piano, harp and percussion, allows the musician to use all their fingers to produce sound by tapping the strings; the possibilities of creating new music are endless in a harpejji. Rahman's experimentation is as vast as his music oeuvre.

His music for *Slumdog Millionaire* (2008), with *'Jai Ho'* and *'O Saya'*, earned him the coveted Academy Award for Best Original Score and Best Original Song. Rahman's musical career boasts six National Film Awards, two Grammy Awards, a BAFTA Award, a Golden Globe Award, 15 Filmfare Awards and 17 Filmfare South Awards.

A Padma Bhushan awardee, this musical genius, often referred to as the Mozart of Madras, lives up to his name of Isai Puyal (meaning, musical storm).

5

BACHENDRI PAL

Nudge Your Fear Aside

*I*f people keep the canvas of their mind free from the dark stains of fear, then a picture worthy of awe and inspiration will emerge. Fear is a state of mind; it's just some random thoughts and phrases the mind often throws up. And once these thoughts and words are ignored, it gives the person immense energy to reach their full potential and achieve great heights.

Fear is a dampener; it drains one's energy, filling one with myriad negative thoughts that have no basis in reality. Fear is an emotion that magnifies the small obstacles until they look insurmountable, making a pebble look like a rock. Though small, fear has a large shadow, like enlarged blurred images reflected by the mirror of one's mind. Several people carry that cloud of fear everywhere. It eclipses their achievements, making them live constantly in its shadow. For many of us, our worst enemies are our own fears. These innumerable fears shrink or expand our lives, depending on the hold they have over us.

It's often said that the only way to kill our fear is by doing the things we fear the most. It's a widely recognized fact that fear defeats more people than any other thing in the world. Sadly, the only vaccine for fear is courage. Thinking never overcomes fear, but action does. Fear is not absent in courageous people, they have just triumphed over it.

When faced with the thick curtain of fear, mountaineer Bachendri Pal chose to surge ahead, shattering the curtain to smithereens. Conquering her fear, she marched ahead to become the first Indian woman to reach the summit of Mount Everest in 1984, inspiring a legion of women to emulate her.

Pal was born on 24 May 1954 in Nakuri in the Uttarkashi district of Uttarakhand. Her father, Kishan Singh Pal, was a border tradesman supplying groceries to Tibet on mules and her mother, Hansa Devi, was a homemaker. The family faced many financial difficulties.

When Pal was 12 years old, she, along with 10 classmates, decided to picnic on top of a mountain. Carrying their lunch, the motley bunch of schoolgirls scaled a 13,123-feet-high peak on a dare. The breathtaking view from the top of the mountain fascinated them, especially Pal. But mountains had to wait, as education had to be completed first.

After Pal completed her BEd, following it up with an MA, her family and friends assumed that she would become a school teacher. But Pal had different plans, mountainous ones at that. She opted for the unconventional career of a professional mountaineer, choosing to do a course at the Nehru Institute of Mountaineering. During her training, she climbed the 21,889.77-feet-high Mount Gangotri, following it up with the 19,091-feet-high Mount Rudugaira.

These two ascents infused in Pal the courage and the confidence to join the National Adventure Foundation (NAF) as an instructor. NAF had started an adventure school to train women in mountaineering, and Pal proved a good instructor. As she climbed many smaller peaks, her confidence soared with each ascent.

Pal's trial-by-fire moment came in March 1984 when she was

selected to be a part of Everest '84, India's first mixed-gender team for an expedition to Mount Everest. At the selection camp at Mana Mountain near Badrinath, Pal came down with a fever and was forced to stay back at the base camp for a few days till she recovered. After her recovery, showing no signs of fatigue, she successfully scaled 7,500 metres on Mana, it was her highest ascent at that time.

The team of 17, six Indian women and 11 men, was now ready for Everest '84, India's fourth expedition to Mount Everest. They flew to Kathmandu in March, then to Lukla, trekked to the Everest Base Camp, spending a few weeks acclimatizing themselves to the altitude, taking short day hikes, interspersed with days of rest.

With excitement and adventure coursing through their veins, the group started their ascent in May 1984. Sadly, they met with a disaster when a massive avalanche at the Lhotse glacier hit their camp at midnight on 16 May. This was their III camp, at an altitude of 24,000 feet. The group was sleeping in their tents when a mountain of snow struck their camp with a deafening roar. The sleepy team was jolted awake, realizing that they were enveloped by a freezing mass of snow, burying most of their tents and leaving many injured. The worst part was yet to come. The injured members abandoned their ascent after reaching so close.

Even as the sight of the avalanche was fear-inducing, Pal conquered her fear, choosing to continue the ascent with the remaining members of the team. On 22 May 1984, few other climbers joined their team, but Pal was the only woman in the group. The group set their IV camp at South Col and spent the night at an altitude of 26,000 feet. The next morning, around 6.20 a.m., they continued their ascent. The spectacle was daunting. Vertical sheets of frozen ice stared at them, freezing winds blowing at 100 km per hour ripped at their clothes, and the minus 30 to 40 degrees Celsius temperature was bone-numbing. Seven hours later, the team reached Mount Everest. Pal had created history, becoming the first woman in India to summit the peak. The date was 23 May 1984, the time 1.07 IST. Pal spent 43 minutes on Mount Everest, 43 most precious moments of her life. The next day was Pal's 30th birthday.

Pal again captured her fear in her palm when she successfully led an Indo-Nepalese Women's Mount Everest Expedition in 1993. A year later, again treating fear as a toy, Pal undertook The Great Indian Women's Rafting Voyage, an all-women's team of 18 rafters in three rafts, successfully completing a 2,155-km-long journey over the Ganges River, from Haridwar to Calcutta in 39 days.

Pal has another first to her credit. She, along with seven women, successfully completed the Trans-Himalayan Expedition in 1997. It was the first successful Trans-Himalayan Expedition by any country.

Honoured with the Padma Shri, Padma Bhushan, Arjuna Award and a Gold Medal for Excellence in Mountaineering by the Indian Mountaineering Foundation, Pal's life is a lesson in facing fear head-on, squashing it and marching ahead to reach the other side.

6

BHIMSEN JOSHI

Challenge Yourself

Most of us avoid challenging ourselves. Seeking the safety of familiar boundaries, we often refuse to try anything new, as the novel experiences or the thought of pushing ourselves into situations we have never been in scares many of us.

Though it's tempting to live our lives while safely cocooned inside our comfort zones, doing the same things over and over again until it becomes a reflex action that we can perform even in our sleep, it's only when we challenge ourselves that we can reach out for new goals that looked impossible earlier. And these lofty goals are achievable only when we push the envelope by doing things we have never done before.

Challenging oneself is akin to throwing the gauntlet before the mirror, the opponent being our inner self, safely tucked away inside the comfortable layers of familiar actions. Challenges not only bring out the best in people, they constantly raise the bar, improving one's abilities, honing our skills to needle-like sharpness and making our reflexes lightning quick. It's often said that if we want to grow, we should break out of the cages we have trapped ourselves in; only then will we end up developing skills we never knew even existed or do things we didn't know we were capable of doing.

Who knows, we may surprise ourselves by rising to our own challenges, bringing to the forefront a hitherto unexplored facet of our personalities! It's only when we take the leap that we give our wings a chance to emerge and develop, facilitating our flight.

Bhimsen Gururaj Joshi, a vocalist whose voice converted every musical note he sang into liquid gold, was extremely fond of challenging himself and emerging victorious. Belonging to the Kirana gharana (a school of music) of the Hindustani classical tradition, Joshi was known for the khayal form of singing. Devotional music comprising bhajans and abhangs was his forte.

Joshi was born on 4 February 1922 at Gadag in Dharwad, Karnataka, into a Deshastha Madhva Brahmin family. Joshi was the eldest among 16 children born to Gururajrao Joshi, a school teacher, and Godavaribai, a homemaker. Joshi was brought up by his stepmother, as his biological mother died when he was young.

Right from childhood, Joshi was enchanted with music and musical instruments. So strong was his fascination for the harmonium and tanpura that he often left his house to follow processions that had music bands. The long walk following these people would often tire the young boy, and curling up in any secluded place he found, he would doze off. His worried parents would search for him, and unable to find him, they would approach the police. As this became a frequent occurrence, his exasperated father found a solution—he wrote 'son of teacher Joshi' on all his son's shirts. The plan worked like a charm, and anyone who found the sleeping boy would drop him back home.

Seeing that the small boy was inclined towards music, his family arranged for his first music teacher, Channappa of Kurtakoti, from whom he received his basic training. Joshi also trained under the classical singer Pandit Shyamacharya Joshi of Bagalkot. Pandit Shyamacharya was a priest. Besides singing, he also taught Joshi to play the harmonium. One day, Joshi accompanied his music teacher to Mumbai, as Shyamacharya had to record a few songs for HMV. Shyamacharya fell sick midway and requested Joshi to record the remaining songs.

As a young boy, Joshi travelled all over India in search of a music teacher, staying for a year with Ustad Mushtaq Husain Khan of Rampur-Sahaswan gharana. A few years later, his search bore fruit when, in 1936, Pandit Sawai Gandharva of Kundgol agreed to be his music guru. Joshi stayed in his guru's house, training with him every day. Sawai Gandharva polished Joshi's brilliance until it sparkled.

Joshi gave his first live performance in 1941 when he was 19 years old. A year later, HMV released his debut album of devotional songs in Marathi and Hindi. In 1943, he shifted to Mumbai to work as a radio artist. Joshi's performance in a concert on the occasion of Sawai Gandharva's 60th birthday in 1946 made the world notice his talent.

Joshi's control over his voice was exceptional; he made the listeners go dizzy with his fast-paced taans (fast melodic passages). His notes, always accurate, earned him the sobriquets 'God of Singing' and 'God of Music'. Using the flexibility of his voice, Joshi would take what is considered the three great ranges of octaves at dizzying speeds.

Though Joshi sang the traditional compositions of the Kirana gharana, noted for its precise melodies, this music maestro used sargam (which is singing the notes of a composition instead of the words) and tihais (used for concluding a piece) effectively to mesmerize his listeners. He often infused bol taans (notes in a fast tempo), which brought in a surprise element in his singing.

Some of Joshi's popular ragas—Shuddha Kalyan, Miyan ki Todi, Puriya Dhanashri, Multani, Darbari, Miyan ki Malhar and Ramkali—often sent listeners into raptures with his pitch-perfect rendition.

Joshi's riyaaz (practice) was tough and long. He trained his voice in such a way that he could achieve any musical effect with it. At the start of his rendition, his voice would flow gently, like a peaceful stream devoid of ripples, then all of a sudden, it would take a gigantic leap for a few octaves, like a plane soaring into the sky, followed by a placid calm like the shimmering surface of a sun-dappled lake, which would continue for some time, all in one breath.

Joshi loved challenging himself by infusing elements of the different gharanas into his music, leaving his individual stamp on his songs. In his singing, there were the bol taans belonging to the Gwalior gharana, the bandish from the Agra gharana, the fast sargam of the Patiala gharana and the rhythm of the Jaipur-Atrauli gharana, all blended into the perfection of the Kirana gharana, with its famous slow tempos of the ragas.

He showcased his musical genius with his novel ways of unfurling a raag. This added a wave of freshness into his songs. By infusing the two ragas Kalavati and Rageswari, Joshi created his version titled Kalashri, a testimony to his musical genius.

Recipient of the Padma Shri, Padma Bhushan, Padma Vibhushan, the Bharat Ratna and the Sangeet Natak Akademi Award, Joshi took the Kirana gharana to greater heights.

Joshi died on 31 December 2010 in Pune. His singing is symbolic of a music genius constantly stretching the boundary of his craft, offering the listeners a heavenly treat by transporting them to a musical paradise.

7

BHUPEN HAZARIKA

Set a Trend

The polka dot, a pattern consisting of an array of circles of the same size, filled with the same colour or different shades, popular with all ages, became a trend several decades ago. The black dots on white cloth is a timeless pattern. Today, it finds itself in a variety of shades, the varied hues giving the pattern a playful look. Though elegant and classic, the polka dot seldom adorns formal clothing, being restricted to casual attire. Its universal popularity has spread to furniture, curtains, upholstery, children's clothing, lunch boxes, pencil boxes, art, pottery, cutlery, swimming suits, ties and socks.

It's unbelievable that these dots at one time had a negative connotation—in medieval Europe, a dot on a piece of cloth was a symbol of bubonic plague and other contagious diseases.

This negative association persisted for a long time, even during the Renaissance. But things changed in the middle of nineteenth century, when the polka dance became popular in central Europe. The popularity of this dance form resulted in the polka-dot pattern becoming popular too. The polka pattern became such a trend that everyone jumped onto the bandwagon, using it in innumerable ways. The French painter Jean-Frédéric Bazille immortalized the polka-dot pattern in his famous painting titled *The Family Reunion*, where two of the six women are depicted dressed in polka-dot dresses.

Down the years, these dots morphed into irregular sizes of different colours, sometimes increasing in size, at other times, decreasing in size but always holding its appeal.

Bhupen Hazarika, playback singer, lyricist, musician, filmmaker and a poet, not just excelled in every aspect of creativity, he set new trends in them, earning the title of a trendsetter. To Hazarika goes the credit for popularizing the folk music of Assam and taking the culture of Assam and other Northeastern regions all over India through his music, songs and films.

Born on 8 September 1926 in Sadiya, Assam, Hazarika was the oldest of 10 children. He inherited his musical talent from his parents, Nilakanta and Shantipriya, especially his mother who introduced her children to *borgeet*, the traditional Assamese devotional songs she sang to them every day in the form of lullabies. With these tunes playing in his ears, Hazarika developed a strong love for music and songs, and Assamese folk music became his passion, inspiring his career choice.

With his father's frequent moves to the different regions of Assam (Bharalumukh, Dhubri and Tezpur) for better employment prospects, Hazarika studied at various schools, doing his initial schooling at Sonaram High School, then Dhubri Government School and finally graduating from Tezpur High School.

It was in Tezpur that the 10-year-old Hazarika, with the singing legacy of his mother coursing through his veins and his pitch-perfect rendition of a borgeet at a public function, brought himself to the notice of the Assamese lyricist, playwright and filmmaker Jyotiprasad Agarwala and the Assamese artist and poet Bishnu Prasad Rabha, who were attending the function.

The two stalwarts, impressed with the young boy's voice, helped Hazarika record his first song at Aurora Studio for the

Selona Company in Calcutta, setting him on the path of music and giving his musical talent a platform. Three years later, in 1939, Agarwala gave Hazarika the chance to sing two songs, *'Kaxote Kolosi Loi'* and *'Biswo Bijoyi Naujawan'* for his film *Indramalati* (1939). A year later, Hazarika in his early teens, penned his first song, *'Agnijugor Firingoti Moi'*, making his career choice of a lyricist, composer and singer.

Post his matriculation from Tezpur High School, Hazarika completed his BA from Cotton College and MA in political science from the Banaras Hindu University. He then took a break from studies to work at All India Radio in Guwahati.

Post his radio stint, Hazarika went to Columbia University, New York, to do his doctorate in mass communication. In New York, Hazarika struck up a friendship with the civil rights activist Paul Robeson, whose song 'Old Man River' inspired Hazarika's song *'Bistirno parore'*. The song became a humungous hit and was translated into many Indian languages; its Hindi version *'O Ganga Behti Ho'* is also famous. At Columbia University, Hazarika met his future wife Priyamvada Patel.

Post his return from the US, Hazarika taught at the Guwahati University for several years, before finally listening to the call of his heart. He resigned from his job at the university to go to Calcutta and focus on his music career, later venturing into making films. He made many Assamese films, such as *Shakuntala* (1961), *Pratidhwani* (1964), *Lati-Ghati* (1966) and *Chik Mik Bijuli* (1969). Besides composing music, he also sang, his dulcet voice earned him the sobriquet 'Sudhakantha' (meaning, nightingale).

His songs, with their earthy and poignant themes, made a strong emotional connection with the listeners, especially *'Parashi Puwate Tulunga Nawote'*, a song about the condition of a fisherman who drowns while he is out at sea, and *'Dola He Dola,'* a song about palanquin bearers. Music has its own appeal, and when the lyrics are peppered with emotions, it gains popularity. Hazarika's songs were translated into many languages. Their Bengali translation led to Hazarika's popularity extending to West Bengal and Bangladesh, and with their Hindi translations, his fame spread pan-India. He also started composing music for Bangladeshi films. His song, *Manush Manusher Jonno*', translated as 'humans are for humanity', achieved stupendous success in Bangladesh, becoming the second-most favourite song after the national anthem of Bangladesh.

Growing up listening to tribal music, its rhythm and melody filled Hazarika's heart with joy, and it felt so natural for Hazarika to incorporate folk music into his tunes. Hazarika was a trendsetter, inspiring other musicians to tap into the rich heritage of Assam.

Hazarika's foray into Hindi films started in 1986, with Kalpana Lajmi's *Ek Pal*. His heart-wrenching song '*Dil Hoom Hoom Kare*' in *Rudaali* (1993) captured the essence of the entire film in its lyrics. His voice added an unforgettable quality to the song, earning him the National Award for Best Music Director for *Rudaali* in 1993. Prior to this, he had won it in 1976 for *Chameli Memsaab*.

Felicitated with the Padma Shri, Padma Bhushan, Sangeet Natak Akademi Award and Dadasaheb Phalke Award, Hazarika was also posthumously awarded the Padma Vibhushan and the Bharat Ratna.

Hazarika died on 5 November 2011 in Mumbai. The Bard of Brahmaputra, as he was called, was one of the biggest cultural icons of Northeast India, showcasing its rich folk heritage to the world.

8

BIRJU MAHARAJ

Pursue Your Passion with Your Heart and Soul

When we say someone has put their heart and soul into their work, all that we are trying to say is that they have put in a lot of hard work. It's also a sign of their dedication and sincerity, coupled with their immense passion.

People starting business ventures or anything new are perfect examples. So obsessed are they with their project that every pore of their body oozes passion and zeal. Whether sleeping or waking, working or exercising, they are constantly thinking of their projects.

Writers who spend years working on their novels, living with their character inside their mind, then putting those characters and stories on paper or typing it into the laptop, writing those stories, rewriting them, polishing and tweaking, are perfect examples of those pursuing their craft with their heart and soul.

Similarly, dancers spend innumerable hours perfecting their steps and moves, dedicating a lifetime focusing on their art. Athletes train for hours on end to qualify for the Olympics. Countless hours are spent pursuing one's dream with passion and fervour.

It's so easy for boredom to creep into one's life and work,

but if one has an obsessive zeal that consumes one from inside, it can infuse a constant stream of passion and vigour, ensuring people work long hours, over years, even decades, chasing one goal or pursuing one craft.

Kathak dancer Brijmohan Mishra exemplifies the phrase 'pursue your passion with your heart and soul'. Popularly known as Pandit Birju Maharaj, he belonged to the Maharaj family of Kathak dancers. Though dancing was his life, he was also an excellent singer, with phenomenal voice control, a superb musician, playing several instruments with the ease of a veteran, and a dance teacher par excellence.

Born on 4 February 1938 in Lucknow, his original name was Dukh Haran Nath Mishra, but he was later renamed Brijmohan Nath Mishra Maharaj; Brijmohan being one of the many names of Krishna. Brijmohan was further shortened to Birju. His father, the Kathak dancer Jagannath Maharaj (known as Acchan Maharaj), was the court dancer of the Raigarh princely state. Birju Maharaj's ancestor Pandit Ishwari Prasad was the first Kathak exponent in India.

The music emanating from the room where his father taught his students fascinated Birju Maharaj in his childhood, as did the dance steps. As a young child, Birju Maharaj often watched his father train his students, perhaps dreaming of the day when he would become his father's student or when he would teach his students.

One day, when Birju Maharaj was three, sitting on his father's lap, he sang the difficult pieces called the tihais (repeating a rhythmic piece thrice with an equal interval between the repetitions) and tukdas (similar heavy bols), which often stumped many adults. This left his father stunned.

Realizing that his son was a gifted child, his father started his training. Birju Maharaj put his heart and soul into his practice, and by the time he was seven, he had started performing at musical concerts all over India, presenting a few pieces before his father's main performance.

Right from his first performance, a solo in Bengal at the Manmatha Nath Ghosh celebrations, the young boy garnered much praise from the older musicians and dancers. By the time he was eight years old, Birju Maharaj had mastered dancing, singing and playing the tabla, delighting the elders in his family, especially his father, who was now teaching at Sangeet Bharti in New Delhi, with his skill in all three. A year later, his father died, leaving the family struggling to survive without a regular source of income. To continue Birju Maharaj's training, his uncles Lachhu Maharaj and Shambu Maharaj took him under their wings.

Within the next five years, Birju Maharaj, with his complete dedication, received an invitation to join Sangeet Bharti as a teacher. Life had come a full circle for him. When India sent cultural troupes abroad, Birju Maharaj's solo performances were the main attraction of these festivals.

As a dance teacher, Birju Maharaj was equally brilliant, training his students with a passion that matched theirs. His teaching stints at the Bharatiya Kala Kendra and the Kathak Kendra resulted in hordes of students swamping the hallowed doors to learn from the maestro. Post his retirement, Birju Maharaj started his own dance school, Kalashram, in New Delhi.

Birju Maharaj's belief that whatever one does one must pursue with an unwavering passion resulted in his mastery of the tabla, naal, sarod, violin, sarangi and the drums, with no formal training or guidance from a teacher in any of the musical instruments. This same belief also infused his singing with a magical quality. No wonder his bhajans and ghazals were considered soulful, and his effortlessly flawless dadras and thumris left his audience spellbound.

Birju Maharaj gave Kathak a new persona with his traditional dance dramas *Makhan Chori* and *Phaag Bahar*, at times introducing social issues into it. The elements of spirituality and culture woven into its narrative as also the innovative music he composed added to its appeal. His dance dramas, though bold, still clung to their traditional essence, leaving enough contemporariness to lure the younger audience.

For Birju Maharaj, riyaaz or practice was like breathing, an intrinsic form of his art that connected him with the Divine every time he practised. Treating his dance like a sadhana, Birju Maharaj considered himself a permanent student who was forever learning at the altar of music and dance, and growing with each practice.

One of the reasons for his excellence was his belief that every time he struck a pose, his eyes saw Krishna, and this evoked his devotion, thereby elevating his dance to a prayer. And prayers are always heartfelt and heart-tugging. Birju Maharaj advised his students that they must treat their dance footwork like an offering to God, paying attention to it and revering it. It's no wonder that his students considered him a teacher extraordinaire.

Birju Maharaj believed that a good dancer must have sufficient knowledge of singing, dancing and instruments, because all three are an intrinsic part of music. According to him, a musician must be familiar with the seven notes, with rhythm, with facial expressions, gestures and tempo. With his complete mastery of all these elements, he set his own benchmarks, elevating his music, dance and teaching to new heights.

Birju Maharaj died on 17 January 2022 in Delhi. The dedication of this Padma Vibhushan awardee to his craft is awe-inspiring.

9

DEVI SHETTY

Think Out of the Box

Many people have this unique ability of thinking out of the box; they think unconventionally and look at situations from unusual perspectives, and the results are astounding. Remember the story we heard in childhood about Lord Shiva and Parvati announcing that between Ganesha and Kartikeya, whoever circled the world three times first would be declared the winner?

Ganesha knew that travelling on his vehicle Mooshika the mouse would be akin to getting stuck in a traffic jam in today's metro cities. So slow would be the progress of the mouse that by the time Ganesha had travelled a little distance, Kartikeya, on his speedy peacock, would have completed the three rounds of the world.

Do you know what worked in Ganesha's favour? It was his out-of-the-box thinking. Yes, smart Ganesha quickly circled his parents three times, saying that they were like the world to him, thus impressing his parents. By the time Kartikeya returned, Ganesha had already been declared the winner.

Another smart creature is the koel, aka the cuckoo. The lazy bird that the cuckoo is, she doesn't build her nest. She instead uses an out-of-the-box solution to solve the problem. The smart cuckoo lays her eggs in a crow's nest when the crow is away. And the crow, mistaking it for one of its own eggs, looks after it. The poor crow even feeds the baby birds when they hatch. Only when the baby cuckoos become bigger does the crow realize that the cuckoo has pulled a fast one on her.

Doctor Devi Prasad Shetty or Devi Shetty, as he is popularly known, is one of the best cardiac surgeons India has produced, who with his out-of-the-box thinking has made his dream of healthcare for all a reality. Shetty, considered God-like by his patients, has made heart surgeries affordable for all. His pledge that no one shall be turned away from his hospital because they can't pay was the catalyst, making him conceptualize a pro-poor insurance plan for surgical procedures. In a country where the poor have no access to even basic medical care, the inability to afford an intricate heart surgery can prove fatal.

Shetty was born on 8 May 1953 in a small village in Dakshina Kannada district of Karnataka. His father, Bommaiya Shetty, owned several Udupi restaurants in Mumbai. The eighth of nine children, Shetty decided in fifth grade that he wanted to become a heart surgeon when he grew up, a decision inspired by South African surgeon Dr Christiaan Barnard performing the world's first heart transplant. After completing his MBBS, Shetty did his MS from Kasturba Medical College, Mangalore, training in cardiac surgery. He worked at the Leeds Hospital and Guy's Hospital in UK before joining the B.M. Birla Heart Research Centre in Calcutta. At the B.M. Birla hospital, Shetty performed heart surgeries for free for poor children. It was during this time that he met Mother Teresa, when he operated on her after she suffered a heart attack. Becoming her personal physician was life-changing in many ways. Mother Teresa instilled in him a new perspective towards his work. Shetty started seeing himself as a doctor healing the humans God had created, fixing problems in their hearts through his delicate and life-saving heart surgeries.

Becoming Mother Teresa's personal physician exposed Shetty to her mission. It also triggered a perpetual drive in him for making healthcare affordable for the weaker sections of society. Health problems, especially heart issues, weren't just restricted to the rich, but unlike the rich, the poor had no access to good-quality healthcare due to their limited funds.

From Calcutta, Shetty moved to Bangalore (now Bengaluru) to start the Manipal Heart Foundation at Manipal Hospital, making it one of the most sought-after heart hospitals. To revolutionize healthcare, especially heart care, Shetty knew that a larger campus would provide him opportunities for performing bigger numbers of heart surgeries and enable him to make advances in cardiac science.

This became the foundation for Narayana Health (formerly known as Narayana Hrudayalaya), which started in Bangalore in 2001. NH, as it's known, with its world-class and affordable treatments, has become a hub of medical tourism in India, with patients from all parts of India and different corners of the world thronging its corridors for treatments. The heart hospital is the largest in the world with 1,000 beds; over 30 major heart surgeries are performed every day; and now NH has turned into a chain of 31 hospitals and medical centres in India and one in Cayman Islands. Credited with having performed more than 15,000 heart surgeries, Shetty's success rate is phenomenal.

Shetty, an innovative thinker, adopted the policy of economies of scale to widen the reach of healthcare. This is also the reason NH performs maximum number of heart surgeries in a day. So high is the trust his patients have in his ability that word-of-mouth publicity is enough advertisement for NH.

Concern for the underprivileged has always been the focus of Shetty's vision. No one is turned away from his hospital on account of lack of funds.

Shetty has constantly thought out of the box to devise novel solutions to make affordable healthcare a reality for all. Shetty conceived the Yeshasvini Micro Health Insurance Scheme in 2003, a low-cost scheme in collaboration with the government of Karnataka, for the rural farmers of the state. When this scheme was rolled out, it took everyone by surprise. It came as a boon for the farmers of Karnataka; by paying a small premium (now a few hundred rupees per year), they could avail world-class health facilities. This resulted in lakhs of farmers joining this scheme, ensuring their easy access to medical treatment, heart surgeries and many other surgeries and treatments. The sheer volume allows for the cost to come down. Shetty's dream is to make India the first country in the world to separate healthcare from affluence.

Constantly innovating, Shetty's NH was one of the first few hospitals to put up electronic medical records on the cloud, enabling doctors to access a patient's medical reports from anywhere. NH has treated more than 53,000 heart patients using the tool of telemedicine, as of 2017. Doctors virtually visit patients sitting in their houses, using advanced technology to view all their reports and prescribe treatments.

Felicitated with the Padma Shri, Padma Bhushan, Karnataka Ratna Award and Dr B.C. Roy Award, to name a few, Shetty, called 'the Henry Ford of heart surgery' by *The Wall Street Journal*, lives up to the image his patients have of him—that of God's representative on Earth or the god of bypass surgeries.

10

DHUNDIRAJ PHALKE

Believe in Yourself

The first thing any motivational speaker will teach people is the mantra 'believe in yourself'. This phrase is both a confidence booster and a motivational ideology akin to staring in the mirror and saying 'You can do it!'

It's also an oft-repeated phrase that one hears while growing up, a phrase that chases people until their late teens. Used as a foundation stone for future success, this belief in one's dream, in one's work, in one's self, is more than half the battle won. And this coupled with hard work is a winning combination. In life, when the lows engulf people from all sides, it's this faith that acts as a morale booster, pushing people forward. If we are confident about the success of our dreams, only then can we take on the onerous task of convincing the world. Because to convince one's self is more difficult than convincing the rest of the world.

This belief is both a thick armour and the strongest weapon anyone can possess. It's also the reason that makes people bet their last rupee on their dream projects.

So strong was Dhundiraj Phalke's conviction that he ignored the naysayers in pursuit of his dreams. With his myriad roles of producer, director and screenwriter, Dadasaheb Phalke, as he was popularly known, is considered the Father of Indian Cinema. He believed so strongly in his abilities and dreams that he pooled all his savings and even sold his household items, cupboards and utensils, to raise money for his project. His family, equally convinced about the success of his dream, chipped in, as did his entire cast, to facilitate Phalke's film projects. In between acting, they painted the sets, helping with multiple chores.

Phalke was born on 30 April 1870 at Trimbakeshwar (Bombay Presidency) in a Marathi Chitpavan Brahmin family. Phalke and his six siblings grew up in a religious environment, courtesy of their father, Govind Sadashiv Phalke, a priest and Sanskrit scholar, and their religious mother, Dwarkabai. Phalke did his primary education in Trimbakeshwar. As the family shifted to Mumbai after his father's appointment as a Sanskrit professor in Wilson College, Phalke completed his matriculation in Mumbai. While he was doing a one-year course at the Sir J.J. School of Art, his family got him married.

Phalke's passion for photography resulted in him buying a camera and enrolling for several courses, learning different techniques and also acquiring the knowledge of processing and printing photographs.

For a brief period, Phalke started an engraving and photo-printing studio, shifting to Godhra (Gujarat) to further his professional photography business. He lost his wife and child when the plague of 1900 struck the city. Post their demise, Phalke moved to Baroda to continue his photography business. Sadly, his photography business wasn't successful, as superstitious people believed that cameras sucked out their lives, hastening them to their deaths. To earn a living, Phalke ventured into painting curtains for stage dramas, leading to his training in drama and production, earning him small roles in the plays staged in the theatre. He remarried in 1902.

Phalke's interest in making films was triggered when he, along with his brother, visited the America India Picture Palace in April 1911 to watch the film *Amazing Animals*. Enchanted with the animals on the screen, the next day, Phalke took his whole family to the cinema house so that they too could experience what he had seen. The cinema house was now showing another film on the life of Jesus Christ; the silent film was titled *The Life of Christ*.

The film made a deep impact on Phalke, and he immediately decided to venture into the moving pictures business, imagining the stories of Krishna and Rama and other gods on the big screen. Phalke now started watching films at night, using a burning candle's light on a lens to project pictures on a wall.

Phalke became so fascinated with making films that he mortgaged his insurance policies to raise money to board a ship to London on 1 February 1912, to learn filmmaking. It requires guts to visit a strange land, that too without knowing anyone there, and for this daring attitude and conviction, Phalke must be lauded. In London, he took the help of Mr Kepburn (the editor of *Bioscope Cine-Weekly*) to meet the British filmmaker Cecil Hepworth of Walton Studios. Hepworth took Phalke on a guided tour of his studio, demonstrating the entire filmmaking process.

Armed with sufficient knowledge, Phalke bought a camera, raw film and a perforator in London. After returning to India, he started the Phalke Films Company. With a firm belief in his dream, he set up a small glass room in the compound of his bungalow, converting one room into a dark room to process the film he would shoot. Within a few days, the equipment he had purchased in London reached Mumbai.

Following the instructions in the manuals, Phalke installed the camera and the projector, shooting pictures of his family members and people of the neighbourhood. Satisfied with the results, Phalke decided to make a short film. The handful of peas he had planted in a pot became his subject. Placing his camera near the pot, he shot one frame every day for nearly a month, showing the journey of the seed from a tiny sprout to a long climber. The one-minute film titled *Ankurachi Wadh* (Growing of a Pea Plant) was shown to a few people. They liked the film and gave Phalke the loan to make his first film.

Phalke wrote a script based on Raja Harishchandra's life. The cast, found through newspaper advertisements, had only male actors, who also enacted the female characters' roles, as women of that time didn't take up professional acting. Phalke handled almost all aspects—from production design and make-up to editing, direction and processing the film. With a cameraman's help, he shot the four-reel-long film in seven months.

The silent film *Raja Harishchandra* released on 3 May 1913 at Coronation Cinema in Mumbai. The film was successful, a big milestone in the history of Indian cinema, paving the way for the future film industry in the country. Phalke, along with several partners, set up the Hindustan Cinema Films Company in 1917, making many mythological films, using trick photography and special effects. People thronged the cinema houses to watch *Mohini Bhasmasur* (1913), *Satyavan Savitri* (1914), *Lanka Dahan* (1917), *Shri Krishna Janma* (1918) and *Kaliya Mardan* (1919), among other such characters and stories brought to life by Phalke.

Phalke died on 16 February 1944 in Nasik. The Dadasaheb Phalke Award, instituted by the Government of India in 1969 in his honour, symbolizes Phalke's contribution to cinema. This film pioneer's immense belief in his capabilities, his motto of 'nothing ventured, nothing gained', his perseverance and his vision gave India its first film.

11

DHYAN CHAND

Keep Your Passion Alive

There is a story that many of us must have read in childhood: it is about a royal barber named Hari who was content with cutting the king's hair and happy with his ordinary life. One night, while crossing the forest to reach home, he heard a voice telling him that for being a good human, he would be rewarded. Thinking it was a ghost, Hari ran home.

Reaching home, he was surprised to find seven pots of gold, six pots filled to the brim, the seventh, half-filled. Hari and his wife were thrilled, immediately deciding to fill the seventh pot with all their savings, his wife's jewellery and his earnings; yet, the pot didn't fill up. They started starving to save money to add into the pot. The seventh pot was like a bottomless well and remained half-filled.

Hari asked the king for a raise. This extra money too didn't help. Hari and his wife started having sleepless nights, worried about how to add money to the seventh pot. A few days later, he asked the king for another raise. That too didn't help.

When Hari requested the king for another raise, the king asked him the reason for it. Hari mentioned the pots he had found at home. The king told Hari to return the pots to the forest, as they were the pots of greed and discontentment and would never fill up, no matter what he added into it. After Hari returned the pots, peace and satisfaction returned to his life.

Seen in another context, the seventh pot of gold, which never fills, is what drives sportspersons—the seventh pot fuels their passion for achievements. For them, it works in a positive way, ensuring that they constantly strive for success. It's this trait that sees tennis players win one Grand Slam after another and cricketers hit boundaries and claim wickets every time they come on the field. For sportspersons, this seventh pot is synonymous with not greed but hunger for achievements.

Dhyan Chand's unquenchable passion for hockey made him one of the greatest hockey players in the history of the sport. Nicknamed 'The Wizard' and 'The Magician' for his super ball control, Dhyan Chand's goalscoring feat was largely instrumental in India winning gold medals in the 1928 Olympics in Amsterdam, 1932 Olympics in Los Angeles and the 1936 Olympics in Berlin.

Dhyan Singh (better known as Major Dhyan Chand) was born on 29 August 1905 in Allahabad into a Rajput family. His father, Sameshwar Singh, who was with the British Indian Army, played hockey for the army. Due to his father's frequent transfers, Dhyan Chand's family was always on the move. This led to Dhyan Chand's education being constantly interrupted, and he finally graduated from Victoria College, Gwalior, only in 1932.

Though Dhyan Chand loved wrestling as a young boy, he wasn't interested in any sport, least of all hockey. On his 17th birthday, he followed his father's footsteps by enlisting in the army. He joined the 1st Brahmans (which later on became 1st Punjab Regiment) of the British Indian Army on 29 August 1922 as a sepoy. Thus started Dhyan Chand's hockey journey—playing regimental games and tournaments, and turning the spotlight on his game when he toured New Zealand as a part of the British Indian Army team.

Since Dhyan Chand practised at night in the barracks, often waiting for the moon to emerge, his teammates nicknamed him Chand (meaning, moon).

When the Indian Hockey Federation (IHF) held the Inter-Provincial Tournament in 1925 to select the team for the 1928 Amsterdam Olympics, Dhyan Chand, playing from the army in the United Provinces team, attracted attention in the first game itself. Playing as the centre forward, his clever stick-work resulted in his lightning-quick goal in the first 3 minutes of the game, impressing the selectors. Throughout the game, his runs, the way he broke through the opponents' defences and his clever passes, pointing to his ability to judge which member had a better chance at the goal, helped him earn a place in the Indian team heading for the Olympics.

On 17 May 1928, the Indian hockey team made its Olympic debut against Austria, winning 6-0, with Dhyan Chand scoring three goals. The Indian team's superb performance earned them a place in the finals against the Netherlands. On 26 May, though Dhyan Chand was sick, he played his heart out, helping his team defeat the hosts 3-0, winning the gold in the Amsterdam Summer Olympics. Dhyan Chand became the top scorer of the tournament, hitting 14 goals in five matches. Newspapers started calling him the Magician of Hockey.

By now, Dhyan Chand was a naik (corporal) in his new 2/14 Punjab Regiment posted in Waziristan in the North-West Frontier Province (now in Pakistan). A few years later, the IHF once again selected Dhyan Chand to represent India for the 1932 Los Angeles Olympics. The Indian team played their first match against Japan on 4 August 1932, defeating them 11-1. The victories continued as the Indian team reached the finals against the USA, where they created a world record by defeating the American team 24-1 to claim the gold medal. Dhyan Chand scored eight goals in that match.

After returning to India, Dhyan Chand resumed his duties in the barracks. A few years later, the IHF again selected Dhyan Chand for the 1936 Berlin Olympics. Winning all their group matches, India reached the finals to face the German team on 19 August.

By the time the first interval arrived, the Germans, who had come with a solid game plan, successfully restricted the Indians to one goal. The Indian team, used to big wins, was disappointed. They returned post-interval all charged up and ready to launch their famous searing attack. The game became fast-paced, with the Germans undercutting and lifting the ball to restrict the Indians, and the Indians successfully countering their opponents with their superb shots and brilliant half-volleys.

When Dhyan Chand's two attempts to score a goal were stopped by the powerful German team, he did the unthinkable: discarding his spiked shoes and stockings, he played with thin rubber soles protecting his feet. He was like a man on a mission, scoring three goals, helping his team defeat the Germans 8-1. In three Olympic tournaments, Dhyan Chand scored 33 goals while playing 12 matches.

Dhyan Chand died on 3 December 1979 in New Delhi. The Padma Bhushan winner's birthday on 29 August is celebrated as National Sports Day in India.

Major Dhyan Chand's hockey career is symbolic of his passion. After every Olympic tournament, he returned to the army to resume his duty. With minimal training and practice, he scored 570 goals in the 185 matches he played internationally in his lifetime. The passion for goals and victories motivated him every time he walked onto the field carrying his hockey stick.

12

Ela Bhatt

Make Self-Reliance a Way of Life

When a gardener finds a plant leaning towards one side because it's top-heavy or has been damaged by the wind or has suffered some injury, it sends alarm bells ringing inside his mind, as the tilt can further damage the plant. The gardener needs to rectify this problem, for it can otherwise stunt the plant's growth.

The gardener either buys a stake or makes one. The stake or the support could be a long wire, a branch, pipe or a wooden rod. It has to be a little taller than the plant. This stake is inserted into the soil, close to the plant, in such a way that though the stake supports the plant, it doesn't damage the plant or its roots in its journey deep into the soil.

After checking the sturdiness of the stake, that it's able to hold the plant's weight, the gardener ties the plant and the stake together with a ribbon, tape or string to give the plant the much-needed support and make it stand upright. The purpose of the stake is to train the plant to slowly stand straight by itself instead of forcibly straightening its posture. The gardener frequently checks the ribbon, ensuring that its grip is intact. As the plant starts to stand up straighter, the gardener adjusts the stake and the ribbon often, bringing the two extremely close together to provide a firmer grip.

Once the gardener is assured that the plant is growing upright by itself and has lost its tendency to lean, he removes the stake, watching the plant to check if it can stand straight without support. Keeping the stake too long can disrupt the plant's growth, as plants need the freedom of movement to sway in the breeze or to enable their trunks to grow strong. The plant must, after a brief phase of support, become self-reliant.

Ela Bhatt, a women's activist and a cooperative movement organizer, has made self-reliance a way of life, not just for herself but for millions of women, enabling them to live a life of dignity, without depending on anyone.

Bhatt was born on 7 September 1933 in Ahmedabad into a middle-class family that laid a lot of importance on education and, in turn, the empowerment that knowledge brought in its wake. Her family considered both these factors crucial for the physical, mental and emotional well-being of a person.

Watching her grandparents participate in India's freedom struggle alongside Mahatma Gandhi in his non-violence movement to liberate India from British rule, the young Bhatt was exposed to Gandhian philosophy early in life, which later became her motto in life.

Bhatt's early influences in life were her mother, Vanalila Vyas, an active participant in the women's movement and the secretary of the All India Women's Conference, while the progressive views of her lawyer father, Sumantrai Bhatt, also shaped her.

Bhatt spent her childhood years in Surat, attending the Sarvajanik Girls High School with her two sisters. After graduating from M.T.B. Arts College with a BA majoring in English, Bhatt joined the Sir L.A. Shah Law College in Ahmedabad, earning a gold medal for her work on Hindu law, a topic that deeply interested her. For a brief period, she taught English at SNDT Women's University in Bombay.

In 1955, she joined the legal department of the Textile Labour Association (TLA) in Ahmedabad. A year later, Ela married Ramesh Bhatt. After marriage, she continued working at TLA. In 1968, when two big textile factories were shut down, thousands of workers were rendered jobless. While visiting the workers' homes, Bhatt saw the women running their households on their meagre incomes. Some women were collecting rags; selling flowers, fruits and vegetables; doing tailoring and embroidery; working in warehouses and in beauty parlours; working as janitors; rolling cigarettes and making agarbattis. These women worked as hard as their male counterparts to support their families, but since they weren't industrial workers, they didn't come under the protection of the state laws. As these women were considered self-employed, they had no health insurance or pension, no regular working hours or vacations, no way to claim their rights or raise their voices, and many of them had to give half their incomes to the middlemen who had got them the jobs.

Pained by the plight of these powerless working women, Bhatt realized that they would benefit by forming a collective union that would work in their interest to make their voices heard and to ensure their access to benefits that their male counterparts received.

As Bhatt had never managed a women's association, she left for Israel to pursue a three-month course. At Tel Aviv, she studied at the Afro-Asian Institute for Labour Studies and Co-operation, receiving an international Diploma of Labor and Cooperatives.

Returning to India, Bhatt, in association with Arvind Buch (president of TLA), started the women's wing of the organization—Self Employed Women's Association (SEWA), a trade union for self-employed women, in 1972. Underprivileged and self-employed women with no fixed source of income now had a union.

There is a popular proverb that says if you give a man a fish, you feed him for a day, but if you teach a man to fish, you feed him for a lifetime. Bhatt firmly believed in that saying. Her vision was to make women self-reliant, as only a self-reliant woman could end a family's poverty and be in control of her own destiny. For Bhatt, poverty was the worst form of injustice and inequality, making people vulnerable to all kinds of exploitation.

Not content with forming a trade union, Bhatt went a step further and formed a bank—the cooperative bank of SEWA, with customized services for self-employed women. The SEWA Bank was started so that self-employed women could get access to the much-needed capital that would further their business and help them shrug aside the heavy cloak of poverty engulfing them. SEWA women deposited their earnings in the cooperative bank, borrowed money to start a small business or to expand their existing business. They also took loans to enhance their skills through various vocational courses, complete their education, build their houses, educate their children or get them married. The bank also provided insurance services. The aim of the bank was to give women access to a fulfilling life that was their birthright. With SEWA's help, these women availed the benefits they would have been entitled to in a full employment. SEWA also had the additional benefits of social and food security, work and income security, better healthcare and childcare, as well as the assurance of a safe shelter. SEWA became a separate association in 1981.

Felicitated with the Padma Shri, Padma Bhushan, the Ramon Magsaysay Award and the Right Livelihood Award, Bhatt, the gentle revolutionary, is a trailblazer, enabling women to make self-reliance a way of life.

13

E. SREEDHARAN

Make Time Your Ally

*B*efore the invention of watches and clocks, people checked the time by observing the sun and its shadows, which changed as the sun moved through the sky. And with the disappearance of the sun and the arrival of the moon and the stars, people knew that it was time for them to retire to their houses.

Some archaeological discoveries suggest that oil lamps used by the Chinese around 4000 BCE may not have been for lighting purpose and religious ceremonies; they may have been used to denote the passing of time by measuring the level of oil in the lamp. Some discoveries point to the usage of candles with markings in the sixth century CE for time telling, though there is no certainty about its accuracy, as draughts quickened the burning rate.

Around 1500 BCE, there were water clocks called clepsydra—devices in which water flowed from one container to another, with measurements marked on both the containers and the receptacle. While considered more reliable, the clepsydra, too, had its flaws—the water pressure from the flowing container could vary. The Chinese modified these water clocks by adding mechanisms like rotating metallic globes and gongs, signifying the different times of the day.

At one time, there were hourglasses to measure the period of time. When the technology of glass-blowing arrived, hourglasses started being made from two glass bulbs, connected vertically by a thin neck—the conduit for the sand to flow from one bulb to another.

With the passage of time, weight-driven mechanical clocks arrived. The first pendulum clock was made by Christiaan Huygens. It initially had an error of less than a minute, which Huygens reduced to below 10 seconds. Inspired by Albert Einstein's theory of relativity, Quartz clocks, using quartz crystals, were developed in 1930. Patek Philippe, a Swiss watchmaker, made the world's first wristwatch.

One person who did the same in India—no, this person didn't invent a device to measure time but facilitated a device (the Delhi Metro and few other metros), saving commuting time for millions—was Elattuvalapil Sreedharan. A civil engineer by profession, Sreedharan is widely known as the Metro Man of India. The retired Indian Railway Service of Engineers (IRSE) officer is responsible for giving public transport in India a makeover.

Sreedharan was born on 12 June 1932 in Karukaputhur in the Palakkad district of Kerala. He studied in the Government Lower Primary School, later moving to Basel Evangelical Mission Higher Secondary School. After getting his civil engineering degree from the Government Engineering College, Kakinada, Andhra Pradesh, Sreedharan worked as a lecturer at the Kerala Government Polytechnic College, Kozhikode. This was followed by a stint at the Bombay Port Trust as an apprentice.

After clearing the Indian Engineering Services Exam in 1953, Sreedharan joined the IRSE. He proved his mettle with his first post of probationary assistant engineer in the Southern Railways by showing his ingenuity in efficiently solving the slew of problems often cropping up.

Sreedharan's tryst with recognition came in 1964, when his boss handed him the responsibility of restoring the cyclone-damaged Pamban Bridge connecting Rameswaram to Tamil Nadu. The damage was extensive, a bridge on such an important route in a bad condition was a huge setback for Indian Railways, and so they had set a reasonably achievable target of six months to get the bridge back in working condition. Sreedharan rose to the challenge, doing the unthinkable, getting his team to repair the bridge in just 46 days, earning accolades and an award for this feat.

The first metro project Sreedharan undertook was the construction of the Calcutta Metro, a project that took years to complete, with no fault from Sreedharan's side. However, it's the Delhi Metro and the Konkan Railway projects that brought Sreedharan under the media spotlight.

The Konkan Railway project handled by Sreedharan is considered one of the most difficult railway projects in the world. It was also India's first big project on a BOT (Build-Operate-Transfer) contract. The project was unique for Indian Railways, as it consisted of 93 tunnels stretching over 82 kilometres, and the tunnelling had to be done through soft soil, which is extremely difficult to plough. The total project area was 760 kilometres with 150 bridges. Once again, Sreedharan rose to the task by making time his favourite ally. When Sreedharan completed the project in seven years, without major cost and time overruns, it was a huge achievement for both him and the Indian Railways.

Sreedharan had his eyes firmly on the calendar when he started his projects. To ensure a smooth functioning of the entire machinery, he hand-picked his teams; there were strict guidelines for every activity involved, from tenders being submitted to them being cleared fast to the on-schedule payments of the various contractors involved, as he considered delayed payments one of the main reasons for stalling of the projects.

Sreedharan ensured his projects didn't suffer from political pressures; he tolerated no interference. In fact, politicians gave commitments for the speedy execution of all his projects. Bureaucracy, known for its snail-like pace, was kept away from his projects. Speed and punctuality became his twin mantras. Sreedharan constantly stayed on top of things, holding regular meetings, taking stock of the work done in the past week, visiting the site to supervise and motivate the workers. Befriending the latest technology was his hallmark.

When Sreedharan was made the managing director of the Delhi Metro Rail Corporation (DMRC), once again, he showed his kinship with time by completing both Phase-I in seven years and the Phase-II in four-and-a-half years, on time and within budget.

In 2009, when DMRC was constructing the Delhi–Gurgaon line, passing through a few Chhatarpur farms, the construction work was stalled, as some farmhouse owners took the matter to court. Knowing that the legal battle would delay the project, Sreedharan asked his engineers to build a station from prefabricated steel so that the project didn't get delayed. Luckily for DMRC, six months before the project's deadline, they won the case. Sreedharan asked his workers to transfer the already constructed steel box to erect the station.

Sreedharan had earlier shown his golden touch when he took charge of the Cochin Shipyard Limited in October 1979, pushing it on the path of productivity by ensuring that its first ship, *MV Rani Padmini*, was built and launched within two years, by 1981.

Felicitated with the Padma Shri, Padma Vibhushan and the Chevalier de la Légion d'Honneur (Knight of the Legion of Honour) by the French government, Sreedharan set tight deadlines, rolling out tracks with speed and precision, becoming an icon for Indians and making metro travel a popular choice of transport.

14

GULZAR

Be Flexible

One of the best examples of flexibility is water. Formless and shapeless, water takes the shape of the container it is poured into, filling every inch of that container. Remove it from the container and transfer it into another, it once again takes the shape of that new container. Water is so flexible that it can even alter its own state of matter—freeze water and it becomes ice, which melts back into its liquid form. Heat water, it evaporates into vapour, which again after condensation becomes water. But, its basic core remains the same; it always retains its essence.

When a river flows down the plain and encounters obstacles in the form of hills, rocks and trees, at first, with its force, it attempts to sweep them away from its path, but when the obstacles prove unrelenting, the river takes a new direction, gorging out its own path.

Another example of flexibility is a mound of clay. All it needs is eager hands to gently knead it and mould it into any desired shape. And then the magic begins. A blade of grass symbolizes flexibility. The reason grass survives the worst storms is because for the duration of the storm, the blade of grass submerges its will to the greater will of the storm, allowing the wind to toss it in all directions. The tall trees standing rigid find themselves on the ground, their sturdy branches broken. This speaks about flexibility helping people in the worst storms. Those who refuse to change with the times are often left broken. It's better to emerge bent at a degree one prefers than be broken into pieces, which can never be put together. People possessing the fluidity of water have the ability to bend at will, and this flexibility helps them leave their mark in the world.

Much like water, Sampooran Singh Kalra or Gulzar, the pen name he is popularly known by, has constantly displayed his flexibility to keep up with the times. This fluidity of Gulzar's writing is the reason his career has spanned more than five decades and is still going strong. The ability to bend at will is also the reason he has worked with several generations of filmmakers, directors and music directors, each with their unique creativity.

Born on 18 August 1934 in Dina in the Jhelum district of undivided India, Gulzar's interest in writing took root in school while studying the translated works of Tagore. Sadly, Gulzar had to discontinue his studies to financially support his family. He left Dina and arrived in Bombay in search of a job.

He did a few odd jobs before he was hired in a garage. This was a blessing in disguise, as it gave him a steady income as well as the time to resume his studies. In between painting the damaged cars, he enjoyed reading and writing. Initially, he wrote under the pen name of Gulzar Deenvi, which he later trimmed to Gulzar.

During this time, he connected with the Progressive Writers' Association (PWA), where he met two stalwarts of the Hindi film industry—Shailendra and Bimal Roy. Gulzar's writing impressed them, and with their encouragement, he started writing lyrics for Hindi films. The successful film *Bandini* (1963) launched Gulzar's career as a lyricist with the song '*Mora Gora Ang Laile*'. There was no looking back after that.

His lyrics found a home in a spate of films. Songs written by Gulzar were not just melodious but also leaned heavily on the soulful, due to the poetic touch Gulzar gave to his words. Poignant and filled with meaning, they evoked a range of emotions in the listeners. The 1970 hit film *Khamoshi*'s song '*Humne Dekhi Hai Un Aankhon Ki Mehekti Khushboo*' not just raised the bar where lyrics were concerned but also made Gulzar a popular choice of Hindi film directors.

The song '*Musafir Hoon Yaron Na Ghar Hai Na Thikana*' from the film *Parichay* (1972) had a hint of the deeper meaning of Robert Frost's poems. The lyrics of '*Tere Bina Zindagi Se Koi Shikwa To Nahin*' from the film *Aandhi* (1975) had the deft touch of the soulful poetry that one has come to associate with Gulzar.

Gulzar was not only doing well but with each hit song, he set newer milestones. '*Hum Ko Mann Ki Shakti Dena*', the song from *Guddi* (1971) had such powerful words stirring one's soul; the song straddled the twin worlds of a prayer as well as an inspirational anthem, and many schools all over India adopted it as a prayer or motivational song. That was the power of Gulzar's pen. '*Aanewala Pal Jaanewala Hai*' from *Gol Maal* (1979) with its haunting melody, expressing the passage of time, became a firm favourite of film buffs.

Gulzar also wrote the dialogues for several films, but the major portion of his writing was penning the lyrics for the songs. Gulzar's writing was dexterous, his range phenomenal. His lyrics '*Thoda Hai Thode Ki Zaroorat Hai*' for *Khatta Meetha* (1978) bordered on life's philosophy of desire. On one hand, he penned the heart-tugging words '*Tujhse Naraaz Nahi Zindagi*' in *Masoom* (1983), and on the other hand, his lyrics '*Beedi Jalaile Jigar Se Piya*' for *Omkara* (2006) were seductive with a brushstroke of the raunchy. On one hand, he wrote the lyrics of the soft romantic song '*Bol Na Halke Halke*' in *Jhoom Barabar Jhoom* (2007), on the other hand, he wrote the lyrics of the upbeat and edgy '*Dhan Te Nan*' for *Kaminey* (2009), a song that became a favourite of DJs at parties. For Danny Boyle's 2008 Hollywood film *Slumdog Millionaire*, Gulzar penned the powerful lyrics '*Jai Ho*', coupled with A.R Rahman's impactful music; it won Gulzar and Rahman the award for Best Original Song at the 81st Academy Awards. The song also bagged the prestigious Grammy Award for Best Song Written for a Motion Picture, Television or Other Visual Media.

Gulzar's lyrics are like water; they bend to the will of the film, matching its tone and capturing its essence. His range is unmatchable; his writing often has deeper subtexts that aren't easily recognized. It's no wonder then that Gulzar has chalked up awards by the cartload. Felicitated with the Padma Bhushan, the Sahitya Akademi Award, the Dadasaheb Phalke Award, five National Film Awards and 21 Filmfare Awards, apart from receiving other recognitions, Gulzar is one of the finest lyricists India has seen.

Gulzar's career is symbolic of his ability to blend his lyrics into the fabric of the film he is writing for. It's difficult to slot him, as his versatility constantly makes his words change shape. His pen continues to evoke admiration for the words emerging from its tip.

15

HAFEEZ CONTRACTOR

Build a Strong Team

One of the best examples of teamwork is the Dahi Handi ritual of Janmashtami, which has its origin in Lord Krishna's childhood. When Krishna was young, he loved the makkhan (freshly churned butter) that his mother and other ladies of Vrindavan made. After eating all the butter in his house, he would steal the freshly churned butter from other houses. The ladies of the neighbourhood devised a plan to prevent the young Krishna from stealing their butter. They started storing it in handis (earthen pots) tied to the ceiling so that the young Krishna could not reach it. This too didn't stop Krishna from stealing the butter. He and his group of friends made a human pyramid (climbing over each other's shoulders) to reach the earthen pots and lay their hands on the butter.

During Janmashtami, this human pyramid consists of a group of people, especially young boys. These boys make a large circle, with their hands around the shoulders of the two boys on their right and left sides. The next set of boys climb over the shoulders of these boys to form a smaller circle until this decreasing concentric circles of humans is near the earthen pot of curd fixed at a height of 25 to 30 feet from the ground. The smallest and the most agile boy finally climbs over everyone's shoulders to break the earthen pot filled with money and curd. This human pyramid is a team effort, with all the members playing to their strengths. The strongest ones stand on the ground, carrying the weight of their teammate on their shoulders. As the human pyramid tapers upwards, the boys become thinner and smaller.

A strong team takes a company forward, removing the dependency from the shoulders of one person. And that's precisely what one of India's leading architects Hafeez Contractor has done. He has built such a strong team that it is an extension of him.

Contractor was born on 19 June 1950 in Bombay into a Parsi family. While doing his schooling from Boy's Town Boarding School in Nasik, Contractor was more interested in drawing and sketching than mathematics, geography and history, often getting scolded by his teachers for incomplete homework.

Though Contractor's sketches of buildings in his school notebooks displeased his teachers, they noticed that the young boy's sketches were quite detailed, as though the buildings and forts were right in front of him. At that time, no one, not even Contractor himself, knew that these detailed drawings pointed to his inclination towards architecture and building design.

This passion led Contractor to enrol in the Academy of Architecture, University of Mumbai. Side by side, he also started training at his uncle, the architect T. Khareghat's company, as he wanted to spend as much time with buildings as was possible.

After completing his master's in architecture from Columbia University on a scholarship, Contractor returned to India and joined his uncle's company, becoming an associate partner in the firm, earning his experience by working alongside an experienced architect. Several years later, he started his own architectural firm.

Contractor's buildings encompass an aesthetic appeal besides the functionality required by his clients. Some of Contractor's more famous projects include Infosys's first software-development park outside Pune, Infosys's corporate educational facility near Mysore (now Mysuru) and an additional building to the Infosys's Bangalore campus. The Hiranandani Garden, a township in the Powai suburb of Mumbai, bears the stamp of Contractor's architectural and design sensibilities.

The Infosys Mysore campus designed by Contractor, with its jagged facades and the fragmented style of its cluster of buildings, looking a bit lopsided, is both awe-inspiring and visually appealing. Contractor got the idea of this building while visiting the site in Mysore. Seeing the contoured, uneven and rugged landscape, Contractor made up his mind that his design would echo the spirit of the site. While studying the land, origami, the Japanese art of folding paper, popped in his mind and he instantly realized that it would suit the shape of the land. He implemented the principles of origami into the buildings, using glass, considered the material of the future, to increase its appeal. Contractor used a ceramic frit for shading the glass.

Contractor's twin-tower residential skyscraper The Imperial in Mumbai is a modernist marvel, as is The 42, a residential skyscraper in Kolkata, and 23 Marina, an 88-storey skyscraper in Dubai. Not content with residential buildings, he designed the stunning domestic terminal at Chhatrapati Shivaji Maharaj International Airport and the DY Patil Stadium in Mumbai, considered one of the best cricket stadiums in the world, and several other buildings.

Contractor has expanded his company from the original three people in 1982 to more than 600 people, getting on board the best, whose passion and beliefs mirror his own. Contractor and his team follow the pyramid method, with Contractor being akin to the boy right on top. He personally designs every project, then hands it over to his experienced senior associates. These senior architects then develop the designs with their teams consisting of assistant architects, transforming the blueprint into reality. All these professionals are assisted by a team of Photoshop experts and graphic designers, with CAD (Computer-Aided Design) operators and 3D visualizers also chipping in, to create the clients' dream houses and offices on the computer.

Next come the site and civil engineers, interior designers, landscape artists, project managers and project coordinators, all working with their eyes firmly on the allotted time and the allocated budget, building the dream houses with brick and mortar, ensuring the impeccable quality of the finished project. At every stage, emphasis is laid on researching the myriad ways these buildings can make a positive impact on the urban environment of India.

From the drawing board to project completion, every small detail is meticulously planned and executed with clockwork precision for all projects undertaken by the firm. Each department focuses on their field of core competence, working with an array of experts to complete the projects.

Social housing is high on Contractor's list, making him work towards his dream of providing a house for every Indian. His towering skyscrapers signify his belief that vertical growth of cities is crucial to maximizing the usage of land. Taller buildings are more suitable for India, with its increasing population and its limited land resources.

Contractor's designs are path-breaking and unconventional, and each of the buildings designed by him bears the unmistakable stamp of his commitment to excellence. His team follows his personal philosophy that architecture must be honest and must respond to the spirit of the time.

The Padma Bhushan awardee Contractor's dream of redefining India's skyline and turning buildings into objects of beauty has resulted in the beautification of the concrete jungles that cities have become.

16

HARIPRASAD CHAURASIA

Where There Is a Will, There Is a Way

A story that most of us must have heard in childhood is the story of a thirsty crow. One hot summer day, a crow flew all over in search of water to quench his thirst. Sadly, he couldn't find any source of water. Feeling weak due to dehydration, losing hope with each passing second and on the verge of collapsing, the crow saw a pitcher under a tree. He swooped down to check whether the pitcher held any water. When he peeped into the vessel, hope surged in his heart, as he saw water at the bottom of the pitcher.

But as the crow lowered his head, he realized, to his dismay, that the pitcher's neck was so narrow that he was unable to dip his beak inside. The pitcher was also too heavy for the crow to tilt it to one side to access the water. Now that the crow had found some water, he wasn't going to give up so easily. Looking around, he mulled over his dilemma. The pebbles lying scattered under the tree gave him an idea. Picking up the pebbles in his beak, he started dropping them into the pitcher, one by one. The water level rose steadily as more and more pebbles filled the pitcher. The crow's brilliant plan was working. Finally, the water level was high enough for the crow to quench his thirst. The moral of this fable is that where there is a will, there is a way.

That if one thinks long and hard, the solution to a problem will always be within reach.

Pandit Hariprasad Chaurasia, flautist extraordinaire, stands as a perfect example of where there is a will, there is a way. Listening to him play the bansuri (bamboo flute), one is transported to Vrindavan, to Lord Krishna's time, the original extraordinary flautist.

Born on 1 July 1938 in Allahabad in Uttar Pradesh, Chaurasia's earliest music memories are the lullabies his mother sang to him, fostering in him a keen love for music. After his mother died when he was six, Chaurasia was brought up by his father, a wrestler, who started his son's training as a professional wrestler in the akhada. But Chaurasia's heart lay in music. He secretly learnt music without his father's knowledge and, luckily for him, his wrestling training built his physical strength and stamina that later helped him in playing the bansuri for long hours.

Chaurasia's father sang bhajans in the evening in a temple but only as a hobby. The young Chaurasia often joined his father and uncle in singing bhajans. One day, the temple priest asked Chaurasia to sing alone. The young boy sang with fervour, carrying the tunes effortlessly and with extraordinary grace, displaying his immense musical talent. When the priest praised the young boy's singing, Chaurasia's father dismissed it, saying that his son was free to sing in a temple but wrestling would be his career, as singing wasn't a lucrative profession but a hobby of the rich.

The dismayed Chaurasia found himself back in the akhada. But luck favoured him in the form of a new neighbour, an older couple, sharing a common boundary wall with Chaurasia's house. Strains of music often floated out of their house. Chaurasia heard bhajans and music, and saw boys of his age entering the house. On realizing that the man was a singer, Chaurasia made an elaborate plan to get the man to notice him and accept him as a student.

Fifteen-year-old Chaurasia frequently circled his neighbour's house, singing loudly. Soon he struck lucky when his neighbour Raja Ram, a dhrupad singer from Benares (now Varanasi), noticed him. This was the chance Chaurasia was waiting for; he had the will and he had now found the way.

Chaurasia became Raja Ram's student, impressing his teacher with his natural ability to carry tunes well. When Raja Ram realized that Chaurasia was way ahead of his other students, he started training him in classical singing. But a disappointment accosted them when the teacher realized that his brilliant student's singing range was limited to the low octave. But he also noticed that Chaurasia more than made up for his limitation with his complete devotion and his tremendous lung power, which enabled him to hold the notes steady for a considerable amount of time, courtesy of all the wrestling training his father had made him undergo by way of long hours swimming in the river to build his stamina.

Raja Ram suggested that Chaurasia find an instrument that would fully utilize his lung power, an instrument with which he could continue his musical studies. Chaurasia's choice was restricted to two instruments: the sitar or the flute. As the sitar was expensive, while the flute was affordable, Chaurasia chose the latter, turning this stick of bamboo with holes, through the sheer power of his breath, into music, enthralling listeners. The flute became his faithful companion.

Later, Chaurasia underwent an eight-year rigorous training under Bholanath Prasanna, the famed flautist of Benares. In 1958, Chaurasia joined All India Radio in Cuttack as a composer and performer. When he shifted to Bombay, he got the opportunity to play in concerts and films.

Around the same time, he underwent further training in Hindustani music from Annapurna Devi, the daughter of Ustad

Allauddin Khan. Annapurna Devi set a condition: to train with her, Chaurasia would have to unlearn everything he had learnt so far. Once again, Chaurasia found a way to fulfil his will. To show his commitment to Annapurna Devi, he switched to playing the flute with his left hand as opposed to his right hand, as he did earlier.

Over the years, Chaurasia played with several western musicians, such as George Harrison of the Beatles, Jan Garbarek, Ken Lauber and John McLaughlin. Recipient of several awards—Sangeet Natak Akademi, Padma Bhushan, Padma Vibhushan, Konark Samman and Yash Bharati Samman, to name a few—Chaurasia gave classical music a new lease of life, popularizing the flute.

Chaurasia's distinctive style of music is a result of his dedication and experimentation. The way he adapted the different ragas to the flute is a testimony of his immense talent and skill, making him the best flute player of all times.

Chaurasia has often said that when he plays the flute, he closes his eyes, that way he ends up playing only for God. No wonder with this kind of attitude, his concerts have mesmerized audiences all over the world. Chaurasia's life is an example of the human will finding a way to achieving its dreams.

17

HOMI BHABHA

Develop Your Foresight

𝓑y developing foresight, one attains the ability to see what happens in the future, thereby becoming a visionary. This has nothing to do with clairvoyance. Visionaries have the wisdom to make a good judgement about what will be needed in the future, in several fields, especially science and technology, and making wise decisions based on this. Foresight also depends on an intuitive knowledge of future wants and needs and being prepared for it.

The faculty of looking far ahead doesn't manifest in everyone. Most people can just see down the road, but people with foresight can see much beyond that—not literally but in terms of their ability to anticipate future events or predict things.

A visionary is ahead of their time, with a powerful plan for bringing major changes in the future. This strong vision of the future enables them to take the necessary steps in the right direction, at the right time. Circumventing all the challenges before them, they move with confidence on their path, empowering their future. Visionaries are blessed with a mind that paints a large and clear picture of their tomorrow, and eyes that have the ability to see beyond the physical world of the moment. Soaring on the wings of their imagination, they reach the land of their powerful visions, helping entire generations in the wake.

Homi Jehangir Bhabha, a nuclear physicist, was one such true visionary. With many facets to his personality, he straddled the roles of a scientist and an institution builder with panache, pursuing excellence in all his endeavours.

He was born on 30 October 1909 in Bombay, into a wealthy Parsi family. Bhabha was an intelligent, hard-working and sincere student throughout his school. His family, especially his lawyer father, Jehangir Hormusji Bhabha, introduced him to music, painting and other fine arts, and this exposure gave Bhabha's personality an extra dimension.

Bhabha did his schooling at Cathedral and John Connon School. After graduating from the Royal Institute of Science (now the Institute of Science) in Bombay, he joined the University of Cambridge, first graduating in mathematics and then in physics. Mathematics was the subject his father wanted him to pursue, but theoretical physics was where his own heart lay.

After completing his second degree in 1932, Bhabha continued his research at Cambridge. In England, while doing his doctorate, he published his research paper titled 'The Absorption of Cosmic Radiation', based on the theoretical explanation of shower production in cosmic rays. It explained the cascade theory of electron and positron showers in cosmic radiation, describing how the primary cosmic rays from outer space struck the upper atmosphere of the Earth, producing particles observed from ground level. This phenomenon of electron-positron scattering was later named Bhabha Scattering. The research paper earned Bhabha the much-coveted Isaac Newton Fellowship in 1934, ensuring the continuation of his research work in Cambridge.

While Bhabha was visiting India in September 1939, the Second World War started. Deferring his plans to return to England, Bhabha accepted a job as a reader in the physics department of the Indian Institute of Science (IISc), in Bangalore. The institute was headed by the famous physicist Sir C.V. Raman. Receiving a special grant, Bhabha set up a cosmic ray research unit at IISc.

While working at the IISc, Bhabha saw the need for an institute for research in nuclear science, nuclear physics, cosmic rays and other aspects of physics in India. The far-sighted Bhabha realized that such institutes would play an important role in the development of nuclear energy in India. With this thought in mind, Bhabha wrote a letter to Sir Dorabji Tata Trust, requesting assistance in setting up a research institute. His letter specified that Bombay would be the ideal location because of the sea, as cosmic ray laboratories often required measurements to be taken at deep underwater levels. Fourteen months later, the Tata Institute of Fundamental Research (TIFR), a collaboration between the Tatas and the Bombay government, was established in June 1945, with Bhabha heading it. TIFR conducts research in physics, chemistry, electronics and mathematics.

Sometime later, once again Bhabha's foresight helped him when he realized that atomic energy would play an important role in India's growth and development. Bhabha wrote a letter to Prime Minister Jawaharlal Nehru, requesting the setting up of a laboratory devoted to atomic energy research and development. Thus the Atomic Energy Establishment, Trombay (AEET) was started in 1954 as well as the Department of Atomic Energy (DAE). Both these institutes focus on exploring mineral avenues for developing nuclear energy in India.

Credit goes to Bhabha, known as the 'Father of Indian nuclear programme', for coming up with a strategy that focused on extracting nuclear power from India's abundant thorium reserves instead of the scanty uranium reserves. Bhabha's strategy led to the formation of India's three-stage nuclear power programme.

In the first stage, a set of atomic power stations, called the natural uranium-fuelled pressurized heavy water reactors, were set up. These reactors, utilizing the natural uranium present in India, would kick-start India's atomic power programme by producing plutonium. This plutonium would be used by the second generation of power stations, called plutonium-fuelled fast breeders, set up for the production of electric power and conversion of thorium into U-233, a form of uranium bred from thorium-232 as a part of the thorium fuel cycle. The second generation of power stations would support the third-generation power stations, called the breeder power stations. The aim was to achieve a sustainable nuclear fuel cycle. In this stage, both thorium and uranium fuel the reactors and thorium is converted into U-233.

Throughout his life, Bhabha refused to accept mediocrity. Excellence was non-negotiable for him, and he wouldn't make any compromises on it. He faced challenges head-on. He believed that the quality of human resources defined and shaped institutes, and he had the uncanny knack of finding the right man for the right job. For the numerous research institutes he set up, Bhabha got on board people who were as passionate as he was. Bhabha also stressed on the role energy resources, such as coal, oil and solar, would play in India's development in the future.

Recipient of many national and international awards, the election of Bhabha, a Padma Bhushan awardee, as the president of the first International Conference on the Peaceful Uses of Atomic Energy, organized by the United Nations in Geneva in 1955, points to his genius.

Bhabha died on 24 January 1966 in a plane crash near Mont Blanc in the Alps. A life cut short at 56, leaving behind a rich legacy. The institutes he set up continue his vision, making gigantic advancements in science and technology.

18

KAILASH SATYARTHI

Let Your Inspiration Forge Your Path

Gautama Buddha, born as Siddhartha in the sixth century BC, was a prince. According to a prophecy, if Siddhartha stayed inside the palace his entire life, he would become a great king, but if he left the palace, he would become a great religious leader. His father, King Shuddhodana, confined Siddhartha to the palace throughout his childhood, shielding the young prince from everything and limiting his exposure to the palace staff. But destiny had different plans. One day, on a chariot ride outside his palace, Siddhartha encountered four sights: an old man, a sick man, an ascetic and a dead body. He was tormented by the visuals. These images not only haunted the young prince but also became the inspiration for him to set off in search of the cause of suffering, the nature of the world and the meaning and purpose of life.

Letting his inspiration forge his path in life, Siddhartha pursued the path of knowledge, meditating under a fig tree for 49 days until he attained enlightenment and found all the answers he was seeking. Once he found the answers, he propagated them through the doctrine of Buddhism, the religion he founded. Not many people let their inspirations guide them, but those who do, not only make big headways but also leave their indelible mark in the world.

One such person who has allowed his inspiration to forge his path is Kailash Satyarthi. One of India's well-known human rights activists, Satyarthi's social activism has put India firmly on the global map. Born on 11 January 1954 in Vidisha, a small town in Madhya Pradesh, into a middle-class, high-caste family, Satyarthi has been campaigning against child labour, both in India and abroad. The motto of his reform is the universal right to education for all children.

Satyarthi's father was a police constable and his mother a homemaker, and their helpful nature, ideology and strong sense of ethics were his first inspiration. Satyarthi attended the Government Boys Higher Secondary School in Vidisha. On his very first day of school, he saw a boy around his age outside his school working beside his father, a cobbler. The sensitive Satyarthi wondered what the boy was doing shining shoes instead of going to school. He asked the boy's father why his son wasn't attending school. The cobbler's answer—that unlike Satyarthi who was born to go to school, his son and other people like him were born to work—shocked him. A child not going to school was unthinkable for him.

Unaware of the caste system and the discriminatory practices of society, Satyarthi burst into tears. The answer was a revelation to him and left an indelible mark on his psyche, making him view the world differently. This incident also became his inspiration, forging his ultimate path in life. The young Satyarthi collected used books, sourcing them from everywhere, to build a library for the poor children who couldn't afford books or didn't have access to them. He was 11 years old at that time.

After completing his electrical engineering degree and post-graduation in high-voltage engineering, Satyarthi joined a college in Bhopal as a lecturer for a few years. An admirer of Mahatma Gandhi, he exchanged his high-caste surname Sharma for Satyarthi (meaning, seeker of truth).

Satyarthi constantly carried the image of that young boy shining shoes outside his school in his mind. The resulting pain in his heart and the urge to bring about a change in society led him to leave teaching and start the Bachpan Bachao Andolan (Save Childhood Movement) in 1980. The aim of this mass movement was to create a child-friendly society by freeing thousands of children from the clutches of child labour, which trapped their childhood in a claustrophobic cage of work. The agenda of this movement was to ensure that all children received free education, as education was a form of empowerment that would prevent them from being exploited. Building child-friendly villages was its ultimate goal.

A major part of the world's population comprise children and youth. This segment of the population in the poorer countries of the world has no access to education, forced as they are to work for a living from a young age. This enforced labour makes them forego the normal activities of childhood, which is the birthright of every child in the world. It also makes them vulnerable to both abuse and exploitation.

Satyarthi's peaceful struggle to correct this imbalance, to stop children from being exploited as cheap child labour, resulted in the Bachpan Bachao Andolan freeing more than 80,000 children in India from forced child labour, slavery and trafficking, with some of the risky rescue missions putting the rescuers lives' in danger. Due to the movement's advocacy in 1986, the Indian government passed the Child Labour (Prohibition and Regulation) Act, prohibiting hiring children younger than 14 years of age for hazardous jobs.

In 1998, Satyarthi started the Global March Against Child Labour, a march extending 80,000 kilometres, through 103 countries. The agenda of Satyarthi's Global March, comprising children and youth in large numbers, was a demand for an international law on the worst forms of child labour. The march received humungous media coverage, highlighting the plight of these children. It became one of the largest social reform movements for exploited children, ultimately leading to the adoption of Convention No. 182 on the worst forms of child labour at the International Labour Organization (ILO) conference in Geneva.

Every child has a right to education—this was the basis of Satyarthi's Global Campaign for Education. Started in 1999, this international coalition of non-governmental organizations is engaged in promoting education for children and adults.

Satyarthi has always been a forerunner where children's welfare is concerned. In 2004, he established the Kailash Satyarthi Children's Foundation (KSCF) to spread awareness about child issues.

As children are vulnerable to sexual abuse in schools, in their communities and even at home, Satyarthi organized the Bharat Yatra in Kanyakumari on 11 September 2017 to create awareness about child trafficking and sexual abuse. The campaign covered the 22 Indian states and Union Territories, marching through seven routes over 35 days, with 1,200,000 people joining it. The Bharat Yatra led to the Criminal Law (Amendment) Act, 2018, with strict punishment for child rape. When the 16th Lok Sabha passed the Anti-Human Trafficking Bill, it was a huge victory for the yatra.

Felicitated with many awards—the Robert F. Kennedy Human Rights Award (US), The Aachen International Peace Award (Germany), The Golden Flag Award (Netherlands) and Gold Medal of the Italian Senate, to name a few—Satyarthi received the Nobel Peace Prize in 2014. His mission of seeing children freely walking to school, laughing and playing with their friends, enjoying their childhood, continues to guide his path.

19

KALPANA CHAWLA

Dream, Dream and Dream Some More

*D*ream big, dream small, dream in the glorious colours of the rainbow, dream in plain grey, dream in white, but don't ever stop dreaming. Dreams are the fuel that drives us in life. Just as a vehicle needs petrol to move on the roads, and electricity is needed for an appliance to work, dreams propel people to reach for their goals. Our dreams can be either gigantic or dwarf-sized, but they should be our constant companions. By dreams we don't mean the dreams we see when we are in deep sleep. These are the dreams we see with our eyes wide open—these dreams become our aspirations, hopes, desires and goals.

When the going gets tough, it's these dreams that light up one's path, giving the person the momentum to move forward, sustaining people during dark times. Every success, every achievement, every discovery starts with a dream. The dream then becomes the goal of life. People who give up on their dreams miss out on achievements. Success is nothing but owning a plethora of dreams.

Never give up on your dreams. Water it with the constant stream of effort, add generous amounts of manure in the form of optimistic faith and watch it grow. It's said that the best way to make your dreams come true is to work hard towards them. Don't dump your dreams into the deep and cavernous underground vault of your unfulfilled desires; bring them out, let them soak the energetic rays of the sun—who knows, seeing these sparkling gems of your dreams, the universe may send you the right people who will then help you fulfil these dreams or perhaps the universe may subtly point you in the right direction!

And that's exactly what astronaut Kalpana Chawla, the first Indian woman to go to space, did. She had a dream and constantly worked towards achieving it.

Chawla was born on 17 March 1962 in Karnal, Haryana. Right from childhood, she displayed exemplary intelligence and imagination beyond her age. During her interview for admission in Tagore Bal Niketan school, Chawla, a precocious child, faced the principal confidently. When the principal asked the young girl her name, Chawla's aunt replied that they hadn't yet formally named Chawla but addressed her by her nickname and said that they had three names in mind for her. The principal casually asked Chawla which of the three names she would choose for herself. Chawla's reply that she liked the name Kalpana, as it means imagination, surprised the adults.

Chawla lived up to the name she chose for herself, all her life. On hot summer nights, while sleeping on the roof of her house with her family, Chawla stayed awake for hours, staring at the twinkling stars in the dark sky. Besides stars, she was fascinated with aeroplanes. Karnal had an aviation club, and as Chawla's house was not too far from the club, she often stood on the roof of her house, watching the planes fly overhead and waving excitedly at the pilot.

During art class, her classmates drew sun, moon, rivers, flowers, mountains, plants and other childhood stuff, but Chawla sketched colourful aeroplanes flying in the sky. Her father indulged her fascination for aeroplanes by taking her to the local flying club and letting her watch the planes. He even arranged joyrides for her in a glider and a Pushpak belonging to the club.

Chawla graduated from school in 1976 with a brilliant academic record. One day in college, during a class, when Chawla was listening to the teacher explaining the concept of a null or an empty set in algebra, giving the example of Indian women in space, as no Indian woman had ever become an astronaut, she surprised everyone by saying that one day this set may not be empty. The words turned out to be prophetic.

While doing her BE in aeronautical engineering from Punjab Engineering College, Chawla chose the topic of time-lapse in space for her project. Space was a subject that fascinated her no end. After completing the course, Chawla, the first woman aeronautical engineer to graduate from her college, left for the United States in 1982 to pursue her master's in aerospace engineering from the University of Texas at Arlington.

It was while Chawla was learning flying that she fell in love with Jean Pierre Harrison, her flying instructor, marrying him in 1983. She also became a certified flight instructor for aeroplanes, seaplanes and gliders. Post her master's, she completed her doctorate in aerospace engineering from the University of Colorado Boulder, joining the NASA Ames Research Center. At NASA, she researched computational fluid dynamics and short take-off and landing concepts.

After becoming a naturalized US citizen, Chawla sent her application for the NASA Astronaut Corps, joining it in 1995 for her one-year training and evaluation. The next year, she was selected for her first flight on Space Shuttle Columbia as a mission specialist and primary robotic arm operator. Part of the six-member crew of STS-87, Chawla became the first Indian-born woman to fly into space in 1997.

After her first flight, Chawla said that on one of the night passes, she had dimmed the lights in the flight deck and seen the stars. Looking at the stars and the galaxy made her realize that she wasn't from any particular land but from the solar system itself.

In 2000, Chawla was selected for her second flight. The much-delayed Space Shuttle Columbia finally set off into space in 2003, with a seven-member crew. During the launch of STS-107, a piece of foam insulation broke from the space shuttle's external tank, striking the left wing of the orbiter. Sixteen days later when the Space Shuttle Columbia re-entered Earth's atmosphere, the damage during the launch resulted in hot atmospheric gases penetrating and destroying the internal wing structure, causing the spacecraft to become unstable; it disintegrated over Texas, 16 minutes before the scheduled landing. All seven crew members perished.

Over the course of 16 days in space, the crew had completed more than 80 experiments. Chawla had logged 30 days, 14 hours and 54 minutes in space during her two missions. She was posthumously honoured with the Congressional Space Medal of Honor, NASA Space Flight Medal and NASA Distinguished Service Medal in the US. In India, several colleges and hostel blocks were named in her honour, so was an asteroid.

Chawla became a role model for Indian women. The girl from Karnal, through hard work and determination, gave wings to her dream of going into space, inspiring girls to dream big and work hard towards achieving those dreams.

20

KIRAN MAZUMDAR-SHAW

Manifest Your Inner Strength

*M*atryoshka dolls, babushka dolls or Russian tea dolls are a set of wooden dolls that can be separated from the middle, dividing the dolls into two—a top half and a bottom half. These nesting dolls of decreasing size are placed one inside another. When removed and stacked in a row, they reveal a set of lookalike dolls of decreasing size. And when these exquisitely painted dolls are placed inside each other, all one sees is the largest doll, hiding an array of smaller dolls inside her body. The insides of each doll are deliberately kept hollow, to be able to accommodate a smaller one.

These dolls usually follow a theme, the smallest doll, which is the baby of the doll family, is made from a single piece of wood. Vasily Zvyozdochkin, a woodcraftsman, made these dolls for the first time in 1890.

If one were to analyse it on a subconscious level, these dolls can be a metaphor for all the traits inside each human—traits that come to the forefront when a situation demands it. In difficult times, people themselves are surprised by how they managed to tide over the trying times. They are often left wondering from where they got the fortitude, determination, strength, patience and perseverance. They forget that a human is made much like the matryoshka dolls, with several smaller versions lurking inside the larger one, which can be unstacked at will when the situation demands.

This inner strength marks the difference between people who survive all the tough situations and those who either fall by the wayside or give up. There is a popular saying that tough situations don't last but tough people do. Tough times are temporary, they will eventually fade away, but tough people survive because they have the ability to become tougher than the situation, to become stronger than the circumstances, making them overcome all the odds stacked against them.

Kiran Mazumdar-Shaw epitomizes the phrase 'manifest your inner strength'. At every stage of her career, she relied on her reservoir of fortitude and determination to tide through.

Mazumdar-Shaw was born on 23 March 1953 into a Bengali family living in Pune. This Indian billionaire is a first-generation entrepreneur, the founder of Biocon Limited, a biotechnology company based in Bangalore. After completing her schooling from Bishop Cotton Girls' School, she graduated in zoology.

Her dream of going to medical school was thwarted when she couldn't get a scholarship. But Mazumdar-Shaw soon overcame that hiccup by following in the footsteps of her father Rasendra Mazumdar, the head brewmaster at United Breweries. She enrolled in Ballarat College, Australia, to study brewing and malting, a very unusual career choice for a woman at that time. She was, in fact, the only woman in her class. Mazumdar-Shaw surprised everyone by topping her class, earning her master brewer degree in 1975.

Mazumdar-Shaw worked at several places in Australia as a trainee brewer and maltster before returning to India. She was unable to get a brewmaster's job in India, as companies considering it a male bastion, refused to hire her, resulting in

Mazumdar-Shaw looking for a brewmaster's job abroad. Luckily, she got a job in Scotland, but before that a chance meeting with Leslie Auchincloss, owner of Biocon Biochemicals, happened. Biocon was an Irish firm, producing enzymes for the alcohol, textile and food-packaging industry. Auchincloss offered her a partnership in his new venture.

Initially hesitant, Mazumdar-Shaw agreed to be a part of the venture. After a short period of training at Biocon Biochemicals in Ireland, she launched Biocon India Private Limited in 1978, with a small capital of ₹10,000, in the garage of her house in Bangalore. This launch brought on a plethora of problems. Banks were reluctant to lend her money for several reasons: she was young, just 25, a woman with no business experience and the business itself was so unusual. The banks also wanted her father to stand guarantor for her loans.

Finally, N. Vaghul, the former chairman of ICICI Bank came to her rescue, giving her the loan. But now new problems stalked her. She was unable to hire people, as prospective employees weren't willing to work for a woman, and vendors showed their chauvinistic attitude by refusing to work with her unless and until she hired a male manager. The first two employees joining her company were retired tractor mechanics; graduates searching for a job showed no interest in being a part of her company.

There were also infrastructure problems. A biotech business required a steady supply of electricity, clean water, sterile laboratories, cutting-edge research equipment on par with the rest of the world and employees with scientific qualifications. Mazumdar-Shaw circumvented all the problems, focusing on her first few projects, which were extraction of papain and isinglass. Within a short span of time, Biocon manufactured the enzymes, exporting it to Europe and America, and moved into a larger property.

Slowly, Mazumdar-Shaw steered Biocon India into a biopharmaceutical company with a cache of products, setting up two subsidiaries specializing in clinical research trials, development of new medicines and generic drugs.

Though Biocon originated as an enzyme exporter, it was Mazumdar-Shaw's foresight that moved it into healthcare, taking gigantic strides by making biologics, which are drugs made from large molecules obtained from living organisms like plants. These biologics drugs include insulin for diabetes and cholesterol-lowering drugs called statins, and have the advantage of less side effects and higher accuracy. Not content with biologics, Biocon strode into the biosimilars (generic versions of biologic drugs) market.

In the course of time, Mazumdar-Shaw became the sole owner of Biocon India. A firm believer of innovation, Mazumdar-Shaw focused on developing low-cost alternative drugs for chronic ailments to make the drugs easily affordable to the masses. The hard work paid off when Biocon became the first Indian company to win the approval for manufacturing the biosimilar drug Trastuzumab for treating metastatic breast cancer and a chemotherapy drug called Pegfilgrastim.

The former chairperson of the Indian Institute of Management, Bangalore, Mazumdar-Shaw has been felicitated with many awards such as the Padma Shri, Padma Bhushan, Karnataka Rajyotsava Award and the Othmer Gold Medal for her contribution to the progress of science and chemistry.

With her personal philosophy that one must work like one's life depends on it, that an attitude of let me give it a shot doesn't take one far, Mazumdar-Shaw took Biocon India to greater heights, becoming one of India's biggest female icons, paving the way for women in the world of biotechnology and also ensuring that Biocon wrote its own destiny.

21

LEANDER PAES

Age Is Just a Number

Age is just a number; if you don't mind it, it doesn't matter. People who treat age as a mathematical figure have always defied the odds stacked against them to achieve the unachievable or fulfil a long-cherished dream.

Most of us aren't able to accomplish everything we want to achieve, as the hustle-bustle of life consumes us—physically, mentally and emotionally. Many opportunities slip out of our hands as education, career, marriage and familial responsibilities beckon. Things get postponed because of the lack of time or the paucity of finances.

Opportunities knock at the doors in one's youth, but sometimes the door remains unopened due to certain obligations, while sometimes it returns in the sunset years of one's life, knocking again. Many people ignore these whispering voices scratching at the doors of their hearts, but some people listen to these voices. These are the people who push aside the curtain of time as though it's a flimsy barrier, to do all the things their hearts desire.

So, when you see a senior citizen climbing a mountain with companions old enough to be his children, rest assured that he hasn't been brought to the mountain-top at gunpoint but is just fulfilling a long-cherished dream. For the same reason, when you watch a woman in her sunset years bungee jumping, she too is answering the call of her heart. And when you bump into a grandmother attending dance classes with people who seem to be of her grandchildren's age, you know you are meeting a person who has decided to do all the things she has always wanted to do but couldn't earlier for some or the other reason. All these people treat age as a hurdle, which they ultimately jump over to fulfil their dreams.

Tennis player Leander Paes is one of the few sportspersons who treats age just as a numerical figure; it has no impact on his game, stamina or passion. This attitude has played a big role in his professional success, making him one of the greatest doubles players in India and the world. The other reasons for his success are his talent, determination and hard work.

He was born on 17 June 1973 in Calcutta into a sports family. His father, Vece Paes, was a hockey player and a member of the men's hockey team that won the bronze medal at the 1972 Munich Olympics, while his mother, Jennifer, was a basketball player.

Coming from a sports family, Paes took to sports early in life. With the encouragement of his sports-loving parents, he started playing tennis from the age of five, when children of that age cannot even wield a racket properly. Paes did his schooling from La Martiniere for Boys, Calcutta, and Madras Christian College Higher Secondary School, Madras.

At the age of 12, Paes joined the Britannia Amritraj Tennis Academy in Madras to train under US Tennis player Dave O'Meara, who was doing a teaching stint in India. This training played a huge role in developing Paes's game.

When Paes won the Junior Wimbledon title in 1990 at the age of 17, rising to the number-one position in the junior world rankings, albeit for a short period, this win not just thrust him into the spotlight, it also paved the way for his joining the Indian

Davis Cup team and turning professional a year later.

Growing up watching his dad's bronze medal, he badly wanted an Olympic medal for himself. His bronze medal victory in the singles tournament in the 1996 Atlanta Olympics has permanently etched his name in the annals of Indian tennis history. For Paes, the Olympic win is the biggest achievement of his life. The match against Fernando Meligeni was memorable for several reasons; a match prior to his bronze medal victory, Paes ruptured few tendons in his wrist. Even with a searing pain in his wrist, Paes played a fabulous game, and the victory was a sign of his fortitude and sheer determination to triumph against all odds and claim that coveted medal.

Paes attributed his victory to 'being in the zone'; so focused was he on the match that he blocked out the pain. This being-in-the-zone attitude has served his career well. Many times he has put himself in that position, blocking out everything and just concentrating on his game and the match.

When Paes partnered with Mahesh Bhupathi in 1994, both were unaware that they would create history in the doubles tournaments, winning six Association of Tennis Professionals (ATP) doubles tournaments, in 1997 and 1998, setting an unbeatable record, which they bettered in 1999 by reaching the doubles finals for the four Grand Slam tournaments. Though they won the French Open and Wimbledon, they lost the Australian Open and US Open; nevertheless, their twin wins saw them rise to the number one ATP doubles ranking.

By winning the men's doubles and mixed doubles at the 1999 Wimbledon Championship, Paes set a new milestone. Over the years, Paes successfully partnered different players, in men's doubles and mixed doubles, notching up victories. With eight Grand Slam doubles, 10 Grand Slam mixed doubles, 43 double victories for the Davis Cup and a gold medal for the 2006 Asian Games mixed doubles, Paes is undoubtedly one of the best doubles players in the world.

Constantly learning, not just from the 95-odd doubles partners he has played with but from life itself, his passion for the game has been unflagging as has been his hunger for victories.

Paes battled cerebral malaria and a parasitic infection in the brain in July 2003, but soon returned to the court, winning matches. At an age when tennis players have long retired from the game, stacking their rackets in their cupboards, Paes, unmindful of the advancing years, was winning mixed double Grand Slam titles in his late thirties and early forties with as much passion and energy as in his teens and early twenties.

Tennis is a tough game; slow reflexes on the court results in the opponents' shots flying past in the blink of an eye. Paes, however, has refused to let age get him down. Considering it a numerical obstacle, he ignored it, tossing the tennis ball high for searing serves, lobbing drop shots, with a deadly aim to get an advantage, slamming his trademark brutal forehands, rushing to the net, lunging a little extra and pushing the opponent for rallies, to win matches. Paes's speed and court coverage is unmatched, leaving the viewers dizzy. He focused on his physical and mental stamina, trained hard, as matches can stretch for long hours.

In 2019, much to the sadness of his fans, Paes announced that 2020 would be his last year on the tour. Felicitated with the Major Dhyan Chand Khel Ratna Award, Arjuna Award, Padma Shri and the Padmā Bhushan, Paes has inspired thousands of Indians to reach for the tennis stars.

22

LEILA SETH

Break the Glass Ceiling

The famous phrase 'breaking the glass ceiling' is often used when a woman challenges stereotypes, shatters conventions aside to forge her path to success. The glass ceiling becomes a metaphor for the invisible barrier preventing women from rising in their chosen careers. These invisible barriers are more often subtle; they are a form of discrimination that thwarts the opportunities a person gets despite their suitability for the job and their potential to rise to greater heights.

Over time, many women have broken the glass ceiling to display their immense talent to the world, becoming a beacon of hope for other women. One of the first few names that come to mind is Rani Lakshmibai, a queen ruling over the Maratha state of Jhansi. Lakshmibai aka Rani of Jhansi not only became a symbol of resistance, she also became a leading figure in India's 1857 Rebellion, inspiring other Indians in resisting the rule of the British Raj.

Many women have successfully shattered the tight confines of stereotypes, letting the cool winds of achievements wash over them by successfully carving their niches in fields dominated by men. When a woman became the first chief minister of an Indian state, she shattered the glass ceiling that women couldn't take the leadership roles in politics. When another woman became the first Indian woman to receive a doctorate of science from an Indian university, she sent out a loud and clear message to the world that the field of science wasn't a male domain, that women could take gigantic strides in any profession, walking shoulder to shoulder with men. When the first female commercial plane pilot strode into the cockpit, it was with confidence that she had not just shattered the glass ceiling for herself but had smashed it to smithereens when it came to women flying planes.

Justice Leila Seth is a stark example of breaking the glass ceiling. She not only shattered stereotypes against women, she nudged every convention aside to make a name for herself in what was predominantly a male bastion—the field of law. All around her were male lawyers, and it wasn't easy battling their chauvinism and their superior attitude. But Seth did just that and went on to win cases.

Seth was born on 20 October 1930 in Lucknow. A lot of her attitude came from her DNA; her father, who worked in the Imperial Railways, was an extremely progressive man. Born after two sons, Seth was given the same treatment as her older brothers. Her upbringing shaped her personality. Her father often told her to stand on her own feet, become independent, telling her that he wouldn't be giving her any dowry, inculcating in her the feeling that she was one of the sons. Her father died when she was 11. Her mother displayed great strength and, in spite of the family's financial struggles, continued her daughter's education, enrolling her in Loreto Convent, Darjeeling.

It was while working as a stenographer in Calcutta that Leila met her husband, Prem Seth, working in Bata. A few years after her marriage, Seth moved to London due to her husband's posting. In London, Seth realized that she could fulfil her father's dream of making her study abroad, but by then, she had had her first baby. Nevertheless, she decided to study further, even as household chores and a small child made that almost impossible. Seth found that the only subject she could study without attending classes was law. Admitting her three-year-old son in a nursery school, she started her law classes.

Seth surprised everyone by topping the London Bar Exam at 27, becoming the first woman to ace it. The London newspapers published her photo holding her first child, with the title 'Mother in Law', a play on the words 'mother' and 'law'. Newspapers called it a colossal waste, ruing the fact that out of 580 students, a married woman had topped the exam.

After Seth and her husband returned to India, they settled down in Patna, where she began practising under a senior lawyer. In the Patna High Court, Seth faced opposition from her clients; appalled at seeing a woman in court, they insisted on a male lawyer representing them. The turning point in Seth's career came when she was pitted against the only other woman in the high court. Dharamshila Lal, a criminal lawyer, and Seth locked horns in a rape case. When Seth won the case for the survivor, her confidence scaled new heights.

Seth's indomitable spirit was largely responsible for her breaking the stereotype that divorce matters or family-related cases were a woman lawyer's domain. She didn't let the fact that woman lawyers were regarded by their gender and not for their merit or ability break her spirit. Shoving aside conventions, Seth spread her wings by fighting all kinds of cases, establishing her credentials with each win.

By now, Seth had completed 10 years in Patna. For a brief time, her family shifted to Calcutta, but ultimately Seth and her husband settled in Delhi. The year was 1972; Seth started her practice in the Delhi High Court, taking up original civil petitions, criminal matters, company petitions, revisions and appeals. Alongside, she also started practising at the Supreme Court.

Seth's hard work and determination resulted in her taking long strides in her career. Her rewards came on 10 January 1977 when she received the designation of senior advocate by the apex court, and again in 1978, when she was appointed as the first female judge of the Delhi High Court. Delhi had its chauvinists, sexism reigned supreme, male judges introduced her as a female judge, people turned up in court in huge numbers to see the unusual sight of a lady judge, but Seth was unfazed.

This attitude followed her for a long time. On 5 August 1991, when she was appointed the Chief Justice of Himachal Pradesh, Justice Leila Seth became the first woman judge to be appointed as a chief justice of a state high court. It wasn't easy to fight the feudal mentality and attitude of the male lawyers and judges of the Himachal Pradesh High Court, but Seth persevered.

A champion of women's rights, Seth was responsible for making amendments to the Hindu Succession Act, giving equal rights to daughters in the ancestral property.

A pioneer, Seth's belief in her capabilities, her determination and courage paved the way for women taking up the legal profession in India. Seth died on 5 May 2017 in Noida. Her life will be an example of a woman striding into a male bastion and marching ahead with her head held high.

23

MAHADEVI VERMA

Give a Free Rein to Your Creativity

When writers start working on their novels, one of the first few things they do is to send their inner editor on a long holiday, thereby giving themselves a free rein of the story in that first draft. The reason the inner editor is packed away to a distant land with a one-way ticket is its constant interference in the form of a niggling voice in one's head, screaming objections that this is not right. The first draft is a love affair between the writer and the story, with no interference from the parent aka the inner editor; the first draft is just the story written on paper or typed into the computer without inhibitions, without any kind of boundaries. This is what pansters, writers who fly or write by the seat of their pants, do; these writers plan little or nothing at all, letting their characters take on a life of their own, leading the story in the direction they want to take it in by flying on the wings of their imagination.

This pantsing allows writers to give a free rein to their creativity, and the results often surprise them. When creativity is let loose, everything one sees becomes the fodder of one's writing, and even the smallest thing one observes becomes one's inspiration.

Hindi poet Mahadevi Verma was a firm believer of giving a

free rein to her creativity right from the time she was seven years old. Her writing, especially her poems, leave lasting imprints in the readers' hearts.

Born on 26 March 1907 into a liberal Hindu family in Farrukhabad (United Provinces of Agra and Oudh in undivided India), Verma, considered a modern Meera, is one of the four founders of the Chhayavad literary movement of romanticism in Hindi poetry. Verma made modern Hindi poetry popular in kavi sammelans (gathering of poets).

In childhood, Verma was encouraged by her mother, Hem Rani, to read literature and write poems. Her mother, proficient in Hindi and Sanskrit, and her grandfather hoped to make her a scholar, and they were the wind under her wings, as was her father, Govind Prasad, a professor of English literature.

The young Verma rebelled when she was admitted into a convent school, and her family then enrolled her in Crosthwaite Girl's School in Allahabad. To a large extent, the hostel at Crosthwaite nurtured Verma's poetic talent, widening her exposure and broadening her horizons, turning out to be the sky where her poetic talent flew unbridled.

The only jarring note Verma's progressive family struck was by following the family tradition and getting her married when she was nine years old. She lived with her parents in Allahabad until her husband's education was over.

In the hostel, along with her studies, Verma wrote poetry, hiding it from both her classmates and teachers. One day, her roommate Subhadra Kumari Chauhan saw Verma's poems. Chauhan, a fellow poet, writing in Khari Boli or Delhi dialect, recognized Verma's talent, nurturing it by encouraging her to write more.

While the other girls played, these two girls sat together, unleashing their creativity on paper, with Chauhan teaching

Verma to write in Khari Boli. They wrote one poem every day, sometimes two if the muse was generous, often reading them to each other. With Chauhan's motivation, Verma started sending her poems to weekly magazines and journals, and the published poems established Verma's credentials as a poet of repute at a young age. Chauhan and Verma attended poetry seminars, gaining confidence reading their poems to a rapt audience awestruck at the two schoolgirls' immense talent. But like all good things come to an end, this poetic odyssey too ended with Chauhan's graduation from school. This love for poetry didn't affect Verma's studies; a good student, she came first in the entire province in eighth grade.

After she graduated in 1929, the man she was married to, Dr Swarup Narain Verma, refused to live with her. It's believed that his objection was that she wasn't good-looking. Instead of mourning her fate, Verma preferred to focus her attention on her work. She started teaching at schools in different villages of Allahabad in 1930. Her hard work resulted in her becoming the first headmistress of a women's residential college—the Prayag Mahila Vidyapeeth—in 1933. The focus of this institute was to provide an education in Hindi, enriching their students' knowledge of culture and literature by exposing them to Hindi literature. Verma organized many kavi sammelans in her institute, and these poetic gatherings nurtured Hindi poetry, giving the poets a platform and providing them the opportunity to reach a larger audience.

A simple woman, Verma gave up speaking in English, she dressed mainly in khadi, wore only white clothes, slept on a wooden bed and never looked in the mirror, living the life of a sanyasini.

Educationist, outstanding poet, essayist, women's activist, Verma played many roles. Her initial carefree poems changed colour as she grew up; moulded by her personal experiences and shaped by her inner pain, her creativity guided her writing. Once Verma realized that her pen had the power to bring about change, she wielded it with a purpose, using the magic of her words to deliver a profound message.

Her poems are included in the Central Board of Secondary Education syllabus for seventh, ninth, tenth and twelfth grades. Verma's poems are marked by the sheer originality of her voice. Capturing the beauty of her subjects, though short in length, they are long in meaning. Her poems *'Murjhaya Phool'*, *'Aa Gaye Tum'*, *'Main Neer Bhari Dukh Ki Badli'*, *'Neehar'*, *'Rashmi'*, *'Deepshikha'* and *'Agnirekha Saptaparna'*, pregnant with pathos, carry an underlying current of emotion, capturing the rich imagery associated with her words. Her childhood biography, *Mere Bachpan Ke Din*, is a widely read book, appealing to readers of all ages.

Recipient of several awards, including the Padma Bhushan, Padma Vibhushan, Sahitya Akademi Award and the Jnanpith Award for her collection of poetry titled *Yama*, Verma's strong views on women's rights are evident in her writing, especially in her stories—*'Shrinkhla ki kariyan'* (in which she highlighted the condition of women, offering solutions to better their conditions) *'Path ke saathi'* and *'Ateet ke chalachitra'*. The titles of her story collections evoke a strong sense of the human emotions residing between the pages. At every stage of her writing, Verma let her creativity mould her writing.

Verma died on 11 September 1987 in Allahabad, leaving behind her evocative poems that continue to inspire and motivate poets to pick up their pens and unleash their creativity.

24

MAHENDRA SINGH DHONI

Channel Your Inner Zen

*P*eace is not just the domain of the sages of yore who had all kinds of potent mantras on their lips or every kind of power at their fingertips. Neither is peace tucked away in mountains or restricted to riversides. It is freely available, like the air we breathe. Peace, called zen in popular lingo, is a state of mind. It's the art of being in the here and now. The art of being relaxed, however turbulent the times, is a rare trait. Sages and yogis have claimed this state as their own, making it their hallmark, perfecting it to such an extent that anyone who is calm is said to be like a sadhu or a sage.

But what many don't realize is that we all can channel our inner zen. It's not difficult. The reason people lose their zen or the reason their peace of mind deserts them, like rats deserting a sinking ship, is when their thoughts take control of them. Negative thoughts have that kind of a nefarious power, which they wield like a tyrannical dictator, often propelling us into actions that end in defeat.

Like a cruel master, these negative thoughts hold the reins of our mind tight, often throwing our mental equipoise awry and throttling our reasoning power. When the plane we are travelling in hits a spot of turbulence or accosts bad weather, the pilot doesn't lose his equilibrium; he continues flying, hoping that soon he will leave the turbulence behind.

We all should be like that. Our inner zen should be on active mode in all situations, whether we are inhaling the heady fragrance of success or sniffing the heavy odour of failure, whether compliments smile at us or criticism scowls at us. Bouquets, brickbats, roadblocks or detours, nothing is everlasting. Here today, gone tomorrow.

Mahendra Singh Dhoni, former captain of the Indian cricket team, has perfected his inner zen. No wonder then he was called Captain Cool. Seldom did one see him in a panic mode in the field. Dhoni didn't scream at his bowlers when they were hit for boundaries, neither did he sledge his opponents. Always calm, he kept his emotions on a tight leash, never displaying the extreme emotions of excitement or sadness when his team won or lost.

Dhoni was born on 7 July 1981 in Ranchi, in present-day Jharkhand. While studying in DAV Jawahar Vidya Mandir school, Dhoni played badminton and football, representing his club and district teams. In his childhood, cricket was nowhere on his horizon. Dhoni wanted to be a fighter pilot and fly planes. One day, by a strange quirk of fate, Dhoni, playing as the goalkeeper for his football team, was sent by his football coach to play cricket for a local club.

Even though it was Dhoni's first time playing cricket, he surprised everyone with his impeccable wicketkeeping skills. After that, he joined the Commando Cricket Club as a wicketkeeper, later getting selected for the Vinoo Mankad Trophy Under-16 Championship. This is how Dhoni's cricket journey began.

Playing in the Ranji Trophy, Deodhar Trophy and Duleep Trophy, Dhoni's hard-hitting batting style won him fans and recognition. The selectors, noticing that his batting was suitable for the one-day games, picked him for the India A squad for a tour of Zimbabwe and Kenya. At the Harare Sports Club against Zimbabwe XI, Dhoni stunned everyone with his wicketkeeping skills—seven fabulous catches with four lightning-quick stumpings in one match, complementing it with his batting. The Dhoni tornado had arrived.

Making his debut in the national team in December 2004 against Bangladesh, and his Test debut on 2 December 2005 against Sri Lanka, Dhoni helped the team to several thumping victories over the years. He showed his mettle in his fifth one day international (ODI) match when he made 148 runs in 123 deliveries, breaking the previous record for the highest score by an Indian wicketkeeper. The Dhoni juggernaut was on a roll.

In a game where a single run or a dropped catch can change the flavour of the match, tilting the game in the opposing team's direction, where two teams are at par until the last bowl is bowled, a calm state of mind is a big weapon, helping the captain think quickly, be an efficient decision-maker and strategize accordingly. This ability made Dhoni a match-winning captain. When a delivery by his bowler wasn't working, Dhoni would advise his spinner, medium-pacer and fast bowler what to bowl next.

Dhoni's trial-by-fire moment came during the first T20 World Cup in September 2007. It was a new format of the game, but Dhoni maintained his composure. On 24 September 2007, India clashed with Pakistan in the T20 final. India had made 157. Pakistan was at 145 for 9 when the last over started with Misbah-ul-Huq batting. He had made 37 runs, hit three sixes and was set to win the match. Dhoni handed the ball to medium-pacer Joginder Sharma, disappointing everyone. In the second ball, Misbah hit another six, the crowd groaned, assuming the match was out of India's hands. A calm Dhoni walked up to Sharma to motivate him. Sharma's next ball was a bit tricky, resulting in Misbah going for a shot that ended up in Sreesanth's hands.

Dhoni's strategy won India the cup.

The ODI World Cup Final between India and Sri Lanka in 2011 will forever be etched in every cricket buff's memory. Dhoni, with his brilliant captaincy and excellent performance throughout the tournament, led India into the finals. Keeping his nerves steady, he hit a six on the last ball, winning India the cup.

During the ICC Champions Trophy in 2013, in a rain-hampered final, Dhoni once again showed his famous Captain Cool trait by giving the ball to a spinner in the last over. The rest is cricket history. Dhoni is the only captain to win the ICC World Twenty20 (2007), ICC Cricket World Cup (2011) and the ICC Champions Trophy (2013).

A recipient of many awards—Major Dhyan Chand Khel Ratna Award, the Padma Shri and the Padma Bhushan—Dhoni is also the first player to win the ICC ODI Player of the Year award twice, in 2008 and 2009. As the captain of the Chennai Super Kings team in the Indian Premier League, Dhoni led them to victories in 2010, 2011, 2018 and 2021.

Dhoni revealed the secret of being zen, saying that while he also got frustrated, angry and disappointed, since none of these were constructive emotions, he preferred to focus on what needed to be done at that point of time. Dhoni's strategy of being able to control his emotions better than others resulted in his success as a batsman, wicketkeeper and a captain.

When Dhoni announced his retirement from international cricket on 15 August 2020, millions of fans were left heartbroken.

25

MATA AMRITANANDAMAYI DEVI

Be the Change You Want to See

*Y*ou must be the change you wish to see in the world—this often-quoted phrase associated with Mahatma Gandhi has entered popular usage and been embraced by many people; some have even made it their personal mantra. There is a sweet story behind it. One day, a mother and her son visited Gandhi at his ashram. As there was a huge rush, they waited for some time, and when it was their turn to talk to Gandhi, the mother requested Gandhi to advise her son, as he was consuming too much sugar in the form of sweets. Gandhi asked them to return after two weeks, saying that when they returned, he would counsel the young boy. Though puzzled, as her son was with her and Gandhi could have easily spoken to him then itself instead of asking them to come back after 14 days, the mother and son went home.

They returned two weeks later. Once again, the mother reminded Gandhi of her earlier request. This time, Gandhi instantly counselled the boy, and the boy immediately agreed to stop eating sweets. While thanking Gandhi for his help, the boy's mother asked him why he hadn't given her son the advice when they had approached him the first time.

Gandhi replied that since he himself was eating sugar those

two weeks back, therefore, he wouldn't have been able to advise her son to eliminate sugar, without first removing it from his diet. Unless and until he undertook that journey, he wouldn't be able to teach someone else. In short, Gandhi implied that whatever changes you would like to see in society must begin with you.

Change always starts with one's own self. Those who practise what they preach are able to start revolutions.

Be the change you want to see is nothing but the call of one's soul. A person who lives and breathes this philosophy is Sadguru Mata Amritanandamayi Devi, a spiritual leader, fondly called Amma by her devotees worldwide. Born on 27 September 1953 in Parayakadavu village in Kerala into a fisherfolk family, she was the third child of Sugunanandan and Damayanti. Mata Amritanandamayi's birth name Sudhamani (meaning, ambrosial jewel) proved to be prophetic; she is a shining gem in India's spiritual sky.

At the age of two, when children are barely able to recite nursery rhymes, Mata Amritanandamayi began chanting prayers and singing small verses in praise of God. An obedient child, she showed a concern for others right from a young age, taking food, clothes and other items from her house to feed the poor and help the needy.

By the age of five, Mata Amritanandamayi developed a strong devotion to Lord Krishna; around the same time, she joined the Srayicadu school. When she was nine, while her seven siblings, both older and younger, were playing games, Mata Amritanandamayi started helping her mother with household chores due to her mother's frequent illness. As her mother's health deteriorated, Mata Amritanandamayi dropped out of school in fifth grade to take over the household responsibilities.

Right from childhood, Mata Amritanandamayi shunned the lure of the material world, preferring to chant the divine names and spend time in meditation. Slowly, as she began revealing her exalted spiritual state, people from far and wide started thronging her house. By the time she was in her early twenties, Mata Amritanandamayi had started initiating seekers in search of eternal truth into a spiritual life. As the number of disciples increased, her birthplace turned into the Amritapuri Ashram. She also adopted the name Mata Amritanandamayi (meaning, mother of immortal bliss), given by one of her monastic disciples.

Mata Amritanandamayi always leads by example, setting a precedent for her followers. Be it the construction of new buildings in her ashram, where she carried bricks on her head, lugging the heavy bags of cements to the construction site, inspiring all the ashram inmates and visiting devotees to lend a helping hand.

A huge believer in walking her talk, when the devastating tsunami struck the coastal region of India in 2004, Mata Amritanandamayi once again led from the front, directing the evacuation of over 20,000 people present in the ashram at that time, wading through knee-deep water to rescue stranded people, working for days in the ashrams' tailoring units in dim candlelight, stitching garments for the people rendered homeless by the tsunami.

Mata Amritanandamayi's views on women empowerment aren't empty rhetoric. She set an example for the world by training the brahmacharinis in her ashram to conduct the pujas in the brahmasthanam temples consecrated by her. Women from the 100-odd villages adopted by the Mata Amritanandamayi Math have been trained by the math in diverse skills to empower them.

Mata Amritanandamayi straddles the two worlds of spirituality and humanitarianism with ease, switching effortlessly between the two roles. Revered as a hugging saint by her followers, her darshans, a manifestation of her selfless love and compassion for humanity, consist of a motherly hug and a few soothing words whispered into the ears of all the people who line up to see her. These darshans have been taking place from more than 40 years, extending almost 14 hours a day.

Taking the words of her personal philosophy, 'It's better to wear away than rust away', to heart, Mata Amritanandamayi has dedicated her entire life to alleviating the sufferings of the poor. The Mata Amritanandamayi Math's global network of charities, aptly named Embracing the World, is a vast labyrinth of charitable activities across the globe, with its focus on helping the poor by meeting their five basic needs of food, shelter, healthcare, education and livelihood. From constructing free houses for the poor and homeless in India to facilitating free surgeries for the poor at Mata Amritanandamayi's super-speciality hospital, Amrita Institute of Medical Sciences (AIMS), in Kochi, adopting 100 villages, improving the lives of the villagers in every way, building toilets in villages, providing them clean water, helping underprivileged students with scholarships and giving pensions to widows, the math is involved in myriad charitable activities.

Mata Amritanandamayi features in two Finnish textbooks for World Religions. The books for sixth and eighth graders refer to her as a charismatic spiritual leader whose mere presence makes a deep impression on people. This suggests that Mata Amritanandamayi is officially recognized as a Hindu saint in certain European countries.

Honoured with several awards, such as the Gandhi-King Award for Nonviolence, Karma Yogi of the Year award, Hindu Renaissance Award and the James Parks Morton Interfaith Award, Mata Amritanandamayi's life is a lesson in humility, patience, service and compassion, inspiring thousands to take up a life of selfless service.

26

MITHALI RAJ

Adapt to Your New Role

Right from childhood, humans enact a variety of roles. As a foetus inside the mother's womb, totally dependent on her for every little thing, the child's movements and actions are restricted. Then, as a baby, still dependent on the mother but now out of the protective cocoon of her womb, the child adapts to its new role of an innocent baby, whose gurgles and smiles bring joy into the parents' lives. This fitting into a new role continues as a child keeps growing. Now a small toddler, fiercely independent, striving to do its daily routine; then a teenager, hormones surging, mood swings, growing into an adult; and from adulthood to middle age to old age, at every stage, the human adapts to his or her new role, making suitable adjustments to their behaviour, attitude and action.

The behaviour of a child throwing a tantrum will neither be expected nor tolerated from an adult. Teenagers have their phase where they go through confusion, but as an adult, a certain responsibility is expected in every aspect of one's behaviour. Nature makes every human ready for their next role physically in the form of bodily changes, leaving the mental and emotional changes, which are more difficult, on the person. Humans have this inbuilt readiness to transit from one phase of life to another, and they can adapt themselves to fit in well at every stage of their lives.

Mithali Raj is synonymous with the trait of adaptability. At every stage of her career, Raj, the former captain of the women's national cricket team and one of the best cricketers India has produced, has fitted into her new role.

Raj was born on 3 December 1982 into a Tamil family residing in Jodhpur, Rajasthan. As her father, Dorai Raj, was in the Indian Air Force, the family frequently shifted from one place to another.

As a youngster, Raj was quite laid-back when it came to physical activities. It's unbelievable that cricket was never the first choice of career for her. To introduce discipline in his lazy daughter's life, her father introduced her to cricket. Raj, along with her elder brother Mithun, would attend cricket coaching classes in her school days, practising in the nets with male cricketers.

Neither father nor daughter knew that a routine started by chance would one day lead her to playing for the national Indian women's cricket team. But as Raj had the ability to adapt to her role, she took to cricket like a duck to water, though all she wanted to be at that time was a Bharatanatyam dancer.

Raj attended Keyes High School in Secunderabad, and post her schooling, she joined Kasturba Gandhi Junior College for Women.

Initially, Raj played cricket for the Indian Railways, honing her skills by playing against the top male cricketers of that time. Raj made her debut in the Indian women's cricket team when she wasn't even 17 years old; at 16 years and 250 days, she became the youngest woman cricketer to hit a century on her one day international (ODI) debut. Once again, Raj displayed her ability to adapt to her role by slipping effortlessly into the women's team, with most players much older than her and some nearly double her age. But Raj was at ease in the team, contributing to the batting score.

The mantle of captaincy came to Raj by default, when she stepped in for captain Mamatha Maben in March 2004. Raj was just 21 years and 94 days old. Raj's 214 not out against New Zealand in Wellington in 2004 made her the first Indian woman cricketer to hit a double century in a Test match.

A year later, she led the team to the Women's Cricket World Cup 2005, gripped by anxiety, with no clue as to how to handle the senior players. Raj, once again, displayed her ability to adapt to her role—in this case, the twin roles of a captain and a batswoman. In fact, Raj grew into her role of captaincy—she read the matches and observed her teammates, studying their strengths and weaknesses, focusing on how and when to use each player to the team's advantage, both while batting and bowling and adjusting fielding positions. Raj was like a sharpshooter, her eyes on the field, constantly gauging the situation to see which player would suit it best, in terms of runs or wickets; she switched batting orders, fielding positions and bowling spells, making many switches that benefitted the team.

Under Raj's captaincy, the team beat New Zealand by 40 runs in the semi-finals, with Raj's 91 not out contributing to India's total of 204 runs, earning her the Player of the Match title. Unfortunately, the Indian team lost to Australia by 98 runs in the finals.

The mantle of captaincy sits heavy on one's head, often affecting the captain's game, but not for Raj—she adapted to the role beautifully. Using her uncanny and unfailing ability to find gaps in the field, nudging the ball stealthily into those gaps, she swept the ball high for graceful cover drives, and when the boundaries weren't available, her quick running between the wickets helped her chalk up her runs. These runs increased, making Raj the second women cricketer in the world to cross 5,000 ODI runs. She broke another record by crossing 10,000 runs in women's international cricket, becoming the first Indian batswoman to achieve this feat and the second woman overall to reach this milestone.

An icon, Raj has completed more than two decades in international cricket, and she is the leading run-scorer for India in all three formats of the game: Test, ODI and T20. Raj had several ups and downs in her career, but with her ability to fit into any situation, she successfully navigated these hurdles. In 2008, during India's tour of England, in spite of Raj becoming the highest run-scorer of the Indian team, sadly India was unable to win a single game, resulting in her being ousted from captaincy.

When she was reinstated as captain in 2012, Raj once again had a tough task of moulding the youngsters and utilizing the older players to their best advantage. But again, Raj showed her ability to fit into her role. This time, she was older and wiser and had more experience. Under her captaincy, India won three Test, 80 ODI and 17 T20 matches.

Winner of the Arjuna Award, Major Dhyan Chand Khel Ratna Award, the Padma Shri and the Wisden's Leading Woman Cricketer in the World, Raj has constantly adapted to her ever-changing roles, making her life a tough act to emulate. On 8 June 2022, Raj announced her retirement from all forms of cricket, plunging her fans into gloom.

27

M.S. SUBBULAKSHMI

Never Give Up on Your Dedication

*E*kalavya from the Mahabharata is not just a part of folklore, he also symbolizes dedication. The young boy belonging to the tribal community just had one desire in life—to learn archery in Acharya Drona's famous gurukul. When Ekalavya arrived at the gurukul, Drona turned him away, saying that his academy was only for the princes of the royal family.

Ekalavya may have been disappointed, but he didn't give up his dream of becoming the best archer. Returning home, he made a statue of Drona from mud and began his dedicated practice of archery. In Ekalavya's case, the meaning of his name, which translates to 'a self-learned person', came true. His mastery in archery was only due to his dedication.

Years later, one day while Drona was training his students in the forest, he came across a dog unable to bark. On a closer look, the acharya realized that someone had shot arrows in such a way all around the dog's mouth that the dog's life wasn't endangered but it couldn't bark. This was a sign of tremendous mastery over the skill of archery. The amazed Drona looked around for the archer whose arrows had done the unimaginable. When Ekalavya emerged from behind the trees with his bow and arrows, Drona was taken aback that the young boy he had turned away was now better than his best student Arjuna. That is the power of dedication; it transports the person to the realm of brilliance. It takes a dedicated student to further the teacher's training.

Like Ekalavya's dedication, which is now a part of legends, Madurai Shanmukhavadivu Subbulakshmi, one of the best Carnatic singers India has produced, too is known for the dedication she showed towards her music. Subbulakshmi's flawless singing bestowed an unexplainable tranquillity on her listeners. Most started their morning listening to her bhajans.

Born on 16 September 1916 in Madurai, Tamil Nadu, Subbulakshmi was exposed to music at a young age due to her family. Her grandmother, Akkamal, was a violinist and her mother, Shanmugavadivu, a well-known veena player who regularly performed on stage. Since her mother belonged to the devadasi community, Subbulakshmi was familiar with stage shows and had befriended famous musicians from childhood. Both these aspects largely influenced the young girl's choice of career.

Subbulakshmi started learning Carnatic music when she was a child, first training with her mother, then under Semmangudi Srinivasa Iyer, while her Hindustani music training came from Pandit Narayan Rao Vyas. A quick learner, the young girl impressed her teachers with her talent and dedication, finishing her musical education even before she reached a double-digit age.

When Subbulakshmi was young, she was fascinated with gramophone records. Rolling a piece of paper, the young girl would sing for hours into it. It's no wonder then that Subbulakshmi's first record was released when she was just 10 years old.

A year later, Subbulakshmi gave her first public performance in 1927 inside the Rockfort Temple's 100-pillar hall in Tiruchirappalli. The 11-year-old girl's powerful singing had a hypnotic effect on the listeners. Two years later, Subbulakshmi performed at the Madras Music Academy. The prestigious academy, famous for its tough selection process, ended up breaking a tradition by inviting a 13-year-old girl to perform. Subbulakshmi sang a handful of bhajans, weaving a spell over the audience, leaving even the critics stunned, as they couldn't find a single fault in her performance. In fact, they nicknamed the teenage girl a musical genius. Subbulakshmi was now well and firmly set on the path of becoming one of the leading Carnatic vocalists of India.

By the time she turned 17, Subbulakshmi had given many solo concerts, and several at the Madras Music Academy, considered the pinnacle of concert venues, where she had made a big impression with her musical talent, grace and fluency. Now Subbulakshmi started travelling all over the world, from the Far East to London, from New York to Canada, giving concerts.

Her career soared after she married the nationalist writer and freedom fighter Thiyagaraja Sadasivam (known as Kalki Sadasivam) in 1940. His encouragement and support was the wind beneath her wings.

Subbulakshmi's concerts at Edinburgh International Festival of Music and Drama, Carnegie Hall in New York, Royal Albert Hall in London and Festival of India in Moscow consolidated her position as the cultural ambassador of India. She was the first Indian to perform at the UN General Assembly in 1966; her rendition of the composition '*Maithreem Bhajatha*' translating into 'O World, Cultivate Peace' mesmerized the listeners.

Subbulakshmi's voice had the power to transport her listeners to another realm. Many considered her voice to hold a divine power. Her speciality was bhajans, especially Meera bhajans. Some of her most famous works include '*Suprabhatam*', '*Bhajagovindam*', '*Kurai Onrumillai,*' '*Vishnu Sahasranamam,*' '*Hanuman Chalisa*' and '*Annamacharya kirtans*', to name a few.

When Subbulakshmi sang '*Vaishnava Jana To, Tene Kahiye Je*', her perfect diction and flawless singing not just immortalized the song, it also brought the listeners to tears. She earned several sobriquets: 'Queen of Music', 'Goddess of the Perfect Note' and 'Aathuvaan Sur' (the eighth note, which is above the seven notes basic to all music), and these were the strongest testimony of her talent.

One thing that never changed throughout Subbulakshmi's career was her attitude to her music—it was devotional, like a heartfelt prayer. Subbulakshmi would start practising her songs minimum 10 days before any concert. Before every performance, she would perfect her lyrics or *sruti* with a tanpura for some time. She never gave up her intense practice and hard work or let complacency seep into her singing.

Subbulakshmi considered music an ocean and herself, a student, and even after she had reached the zenith of success, she continued her daily practice with dedication. She took no chances, preferring to adopt the attitude of being a learner all her life. When singing in an unfamiliar language, Subbulakshmi spent a lot of time delving into the meaning of the words and the song itself, mastering the correct pronunciation of each word of the song or bhajan. She endorsed voice practice, always working hard to perfect her diction, often spending months learning Sanskrit texts so that she had a better understanding of the songs she was singing.

The musical genius was felicitated with many awards, such as the Padma Bhushan, Sangeet Natak Akademi Award, Sangeetha Kalanidhi, Padma Vibhushan, Sangeetha Kalasikhamani, Kalidas Samman and the Indira Gandhi Award for National Integration. She was the first musician to receive the Bharat Ratna and the Ramon Magsaysay Award. Subbulakshmi sang her way into the hearts of her listeners, and her entire life is a lesson in dedication to one's craft.

28

M.S. SWAMINATHAN

Align with a Vision

When one thinks of the phrase 'aligning with a vision', the first thing that comes to many minds is the image of a railway track, stretching on and on. The two tracks have come together for a cause—for facilitating the movement of hundreds of trains on a daily basis. They have aligned with each other in such a way that their coming together benefits humans in a huge way. Though the tracks will never meet (in this case, it's better they don't), their common vision makes them come together for that purpose—of making land travel possible. It's because they came together that their cause came to fruition.

Aligning could also be a sign of acceptance or adherence to certain rules. When the lights in the theatre are switched off, the audience knows that the film is about to start. People put their mobile phones on silent modes, turn towards the big screen and sit up straight in their seats. Their actions are indicative of their tacit support of the rules of the theatre, showing that they have aligned with those rules. Aligning actions are important, as they denote to everyone that people will behave in a way that is normal. These can be common ones like waiting in queues at a supermarket, theatres and stadiums in an orderly way or leaving a classroom after the bell and heading towards the next one.

Uniforms are a sign of aligning with the cause of school education. Well, whatever forms these aligning actions take, they all end up showing others that we agree with the norms and expectations of a given situation and that we will act in accordance with it.

It was due to Mankombu Sambasivan Swaminathan or M.S. Swaminathan aligning with the vision of ridding the world of hunger by helping farmers produce more wheat that the Green Revolution happened in India. This aligning with his vision not just made Swaminathan's goal easy but also earned him the title of Father of the Green Revolution.

Swaminathan was born on 7 August 1925 in Kumbakonam, Tamil Nadu. From a young age, his father, Dr M.K. Sambasivan, a surgeon, instilled in him the belief that anything in life could be achieved through one's will and effort. One of Swaminathan's major inspirations and influences was Mahatma Gandhi, courtesy of his father who was a big follower of Gandhi and a supporter of his Swadeshi movement. In childhood, oscillating between two career choices of a police officer and a doctor, Swaminathan was sure of one thing—he wanted to serve his country.

After his father's death when he was 11 years old, Swaminathan was brought up by his uncle, M.K. Narayanaswami, a radiologist. Swaminathan completed his schooling from Catholic Little Flower High School in Kumbakonam. When he was in his late teens, following his father's footsteps, Swaminathan enrolled for medicine at the University of Kerala. Around the same time, the Great Bengal Famine ravaged parts of India in 1943. An acute shortage of rice resulted in millions of people dying of starvation in Bengal. During this time, Swaminathan was an active participant in Gandhi's freedom movement, which had intensified its efforts to free India from British rule.

Seeing the famine and its devastating effects on the population, Swaminathan decided to undertake agricultural research to help farmers produce more crops. For this reason, he switched from his medical course to the agricultural and allied fields, first graduating in zoology, but not being satisfied with one degree, going on to pursue a second BSc degree in agricultural science. He followed it up with a postgraduate degree from the Indian Agricultural Research Institute (IARI), studying plant breeding and genetics.

After he won a fellowship in 1949, he studied agriculture in the Netherlands and the United Kingdom. Post his doctorate in plant genetics from Cambridge University, he continued his research abroad. But a dissatisfaction and restlessness assailed him. His desire was to work towards solving the issue of low food production in India and trying to avert a food crisis that India's burgeoning population was heading towards.

Returning to India, he joined IARI as a scientist. It was during his stint with IARI that Swaminathan heard about American agronomist Dr Norman Borlaug's initiatives and also about his newly developed semi-dwarf, high-yield and disease-resistant variety of wheat. Dr Borlaug visited India on Swaminathan's invitation, and the two scientists worked together to develop varieties of wheat that would yield higher produce. Their endeavour was to develop a strain of wheat with strong stalks that could support the increased biomass. Their hard work and dedication paid off when they achieved this scientific breakthrough.

Not content with just developing a variety of higher-yielding wheat, Swaminathan wanted to take this scientific knowledge to the farmers, to the people whom it would affect the most, and through them, benefit the country. The year was 1965. For this purpose, Swaminathan and his team visited the northern regions of India, setting up test plots everywhere, demonstrating to the hesitant farmers how they could benefit from sowing these genetically improved wheat grain in their small fields. The result was a harvest three times more than the previous years. The farmers greatly benefitted from this direct contact with Swaminathan, as they learned new farming techniques that became a part of modern agriculture. Swaminathan had now earned the farmer's trust and complete admiration.

Swaminathan's research also extended to potato, rice and jute. Under the aegis of his Green Revolution programme, high-yielding varieties of wheat and rice saplings were distributed to farmers all over India. By choosing the career of a plant geneticist, Swaminathan aligned with the clear goal in his mind—of making India self-sufficient in grain production, especially wheat and rice, and eliminating hunger. His focus was also to conserve natural resources and the biodiversity of India through sustainable agriculture, which used groundbreaking innovations in ecotechnology.

Swaminathan was feted with the Padma Shri, Padma Bhushan, the Ramon Magsaysay Award for Community Leadership and the Albert Einstein World Award of Science, as a recognition for his contributions to plant genetics and agricultural development.

Swaminathan started the MS Swaminathan Research Foundation in Madras in 1988 with the World Food Prize award money he received. His belief that research should reach the unreached has been instrumental in ending India's reliance on imports for grains and ensuring food security for our country. Swaminathan's contribution to agricultural science earned him the sobriquet Father of Economic Ecology.

29

NANDALAL BOSE

Find Your Groove

*I*t's not always possible to find one's groove right at the first instance or in the first thing one does. For some people, several career switches happen before they are able to settle down into a comfortable zone. People who haven't found their groove are assailed by a kind of restlessness and dissatisfaction. Though everything looks perfect on the surface, they still feel something is lacking or missing in their lives or careers, something they are unable to pinpoint. And this is the reason why, many times, they aren't able to give their best at all.

It's for the same reason that some people, after studying engineering and working in the IT sector for several years, switch track, becoming food entrepreneurs. They find satisfaction in whipping up dishes instead of coding. For the same reason, a person who has studied medicine sometimes decides to exchange the stethoscope for a pen, becoming a writer. Likewise for an architect who exchanges the blueprints for a blackboard, as teaching underprivileged children is way more rewarding than designing buildings. All these people found their groove in professions they had no connection with, in subjects they hadn't studied. One never knows in which profession one's ultimate calling in life lies.

The popular KFC logo of a smiling man in a red apron is Harland David Sanders or Colonel Sanders, who, after trying several jobs, such as farming, streetcar conductor, steamboat operator, railroad fireman and insurance salesman, found his groove in the kitchen, creating a yummy fried chicken recipe, launching one of the world's best fast-food chain of restaurants called the Kentucky Fried Chicken aka KFC.

Called the Artist Laureate of India, Nandalal Bose, one of the most celebrated Indian painters of the twentieth century, found his groove in the rural scenes he painted, pioneering the Indian modern art movement in India by nudging the Indian art scene away from the western influences creeping into it. Indian art before the partition of India was heavily imbued with the styles of western artists.

Bose was born on 3 December 1882 in Kharagpur (Bengal Presidency) into a middle-class Bengali family. Bose's father, Purnachandra, worked as a manager for the maharaja of Darbhanga, and his homemaker mother, Kshetramonidevi, had a passion for making unusual toys and dolls for her five children. The Bose family lived in an area surrounded by potters and idol-makers. Bose's artistic genius found its inspiration in both his mother's handicrafts and the craftmen's creations, instilling in the young boy a keen interest and a love for the crafts. Bose often made small images for Durga Puja, decorating the puja pandals.

In school, Bose filled his notebooks with sketches of gods and goddesses, while his classmates copied down their notes. The young boy had less interest in his studies and more interest in art. His parents forced him to concentrate on his education, sending him to study in the Central Collegiate School in Calcutta when he was 15.

With a complete disinterest in commerce, the subject he was pursuing in college, Bose often failed in his studies, much to his family's dismay. This resulted in him moving from one college to another. By now, Bose was married to Sudhira Devi. It was while Bose was studying in the Presidency College that he secretly started learning painting from his cousin Atul Mitra, honing his skills in still-life painting, model painting and sauce painting. His family finally allowed him to join the Government College of Art and Craft in Calcutta.

Bose was an admirer of Abanindranath Tagore, and keen to train under him, he visited the famous painter with a few of his paintings. Impressed with his skills, Tagore accepted him as his pupil, training him for five years. When the Indian Society of Oriental Art organized an exhibition, Bose displayed two of his paintings, *Sati* and *Siva and Sati*, winning ₹500 as the prize. Bose had big plans for this princely sum; he used it to travel all over India, seeing the myriad Indian art forms, especially the murals of the Ajanta Caves, which found representation in his paintings.

Bose found his groove in rustic themes; his art had an earthy appeal—one, for the subjects, and two, for the colours he used. Drawing inspiration from life, Bose's paintings focused on the relationship between man and nature. His light brown and grey painting of *Sabari in her Youth*, a tribal woman climbing a tree, the dull landscape (symbolic of her long wait) stretching to the distant horizon, was inspired by an incident in the Ramayana. Another painting titled *Mother Bathing her Child*, with its poignant portrayal of a mother giving her child a bath, reminded people of Krishna and Yashoda. The painting titled *A Washerman*, with its two subjects—a washerman and his donkey, carrying the bundle of clothes, was an interplay of various shades of brown interspersed with the white of the bundle of cloth. *Yama and Savitri*, with its stark portrayal of Savitri stalking Yama, transmitted the grimness of the scene. Bose's paintings were marked by his clear palettes; the figures were bold; and the hues restricted to browns, greys, whites and blacks. With his original style, Bose won over both the art lovers as well as critics all over the world.

At the invitation of Rabindranath Tagore, the founder of Santiniketan, Bose joined Kala Bhavan in 1920 as a teacher, later serving as the principal from 1922 to 1951. Bose's paintings came under the limelight when he painted a linocut of Mahatma Gandhi's Dandi March (a protest against salt tax). This black-on-white painting of Gandhi marching with his staff became symbolic of the non-violence movement.

After India's independence, Bose received his ultimate honour when Prime Minister Jawaharlal Nehru requested Bose to design the emblems for the two awards, the Bharat Ratna and the Padma Shri. For the Bharat Ratna, Bose crafted a medal in the shape of a peepal leaf, on one side is the image of the sun with the words 'Bharat Ratna' in Devanagari script and on the other side is the State Emblem of India with Satyameva Jayate written in Devanagari script. Bose also beautified the original manuscript of the Constitution of India.

The Indian government declared Bose's paintings as art treasures, a true testimony to their artistic genius and value as national treasures. Most of his 7,000-odd paintings decorate the walls of the National Gallery of Modern Art in New Delhi, delighting art lovers.

Bose died on 16 April 1966 in Calcutta. Elected Fellow of the Lalit Kala Akademi, this Padma Vibhushan awardee's faith in his ability ensured that he followed his passion against all objections from his family, going on to find his groove.

30

N.R. NARAYANA MURTHY

Treat Failure as a By-Product of Success

Failure—which beast is that? All the people who have thought along these lines have literally shoved failure aside, meeting with thumping success, the sound of their achievements resounding for years together, going on to inspire generations. A lot depends on us—whether we treat failure as a scary monster out to devour us or as a friendly ghost with an irritating presence who we will encounter repeatedly on our path to success.

If we treat failure as it rightfully deserves to be treated, as one of the many faltering steps towards that ultimate shiny goal called success, we start seeing it in a different light. If we let failure affect our heart, it will suck out our passion and drain us of our energy. To keep the fire of passion burning bright and long, it's important to not let the fatal air of failure anywhere near it. Not even a whiff.

Most successful people have failed many times, but what differentiates them and makes them achievers is their ability to not let their failure hold them back from trying repeatedly. A child learning to walk falls every time he or she stands up. But does the child give up? No. The determination overrides failure, resulting in ultimate success.

Success is rarely easy. For every invention or discovery, the creator undergoes heartbreak and hardships, encountering recurring failure, but those who keep moving ahead are the ones who reach the finish line of success.

When people taunted American inventor Thomas Edison about his many attempts to make a light bulb, he replied, 'I have not failed, I have just found 10,000 ways that won't work.' Needless to say, Edison went on to invent the long-lasting, practical electric light bulb. If Edison had given up after he had encountered the first lot of failures, there would have been no light bulb.

Thankfully, Nagavara Ramarao Narayana Murthy didn't let the failure of the first company he set up deter him. If that had happened, there would have been no Infosys. For that we have to thank Murthy and the other co-founders of Infosys, a company that put India firmly on the global map.

Born on 20 August 1946 in Shidlaghatta, Karnataka, Murthy was academically brilliant from his school days, passionate about mathematics and physics, with big dreams of starting his own venture. After graduating in electrical engineering from the National Institute of Engineering, Mysore, he did his master's from the Indian Institute of Technology, Kanpur.

Before Infosys was anywhere on Murthy's radar, he worked at IIM Ahmedabad as a research associate with a faculty member, later becoming the chief systems programmer working on India's first time-sharing computer system. Always enterprising, Murthy also designed and implemented a BASIC computer interpreter for the Electronic Corporation of India Limited.

Perhaps this success gave him the impetus to start his own company, Softronics, a software consulting firm. One-and-a-half years later, Softronics was still floundering and met with failure. A bit disappointed, Murthy moved on to his plan B by joining Patni Computer Systems in Pune. The plan B turned out to be a blessing in disguise. It was while he was working with Patni Computers, as a systems programmer, that Murthy met his future co-partners. Together with several of his colleagues—Nandan Nilekani, N.S. Raghavan, S. Gopalakrishnan, S.D. Shibulal, K. Dinesh and Ashok Arora—he started Infosys. None of the founders had a business background or surplus funds; they just had a passion to create world-class software, a will to work hard and a determination to achieve their dream.

Murthy didn't let the failure of Softronics affect his dream of starting his own company. Infosys Consultants Private Limited, as it was then called, saw its birth in Pune in 1981 with a small initial capital of ₹10,000, which Murthy borrowed from his wife Sudha, while the Murthy residence became the company's first office. Both these facts are now a part of business legends and have been the inspiration behind many start-ups.

It wasn't all smooth sailing for the founders of Infosys; the initial struggles were long and hard, the business environment in India wasn't friendly. It took Murthy a year to complete his work at Patni Computers before he could join his own company, and by the time he joined, he was the fourth employee.

If one were to think that as Infosys had started, success was chasing it, it would be a mistake. Still more hurdles awaited Murthy and the other founders. The company didn't have a computer because the founders couldn't afford to buy an imported one they all had liked. Lack of a computer is a huge roadblock for a software company. Nevertheless, the founders ploughed on with their dream. Two years later, they finally managed to buy a computer, a 32-bit Data General Eclipse MV/8000.

Though the company was now on the right path, more problems awaited the founders. A company needs all kinds of specialists, and it wasn't easy for the founders with an expertise in designing, writing and testing codes to run a business. With a focus on the global market, Infosys formed a joint venture partnership with Kurt Salmon Associates, called KSA-Infosys. And when it collapsed in 1989, Infosys was badly affected and left in a lurch. Facing its first major crisis, the company was also on the verge of a collapse. More anguish followed when one of the founders, Ashok Arora, disillusioned with the way things were going, decided to quit.

At that point, Murthy, backed by his conviction and belief in his vision, announced to the remaining founders that if they wanted to leave, they could do so, but he would stay put and make it work. Perhaps inspired by Murthy's conviction, the remaining partners—Nilekani, Gopalakrishnan, Dinesh, Raghavan and Shibulal—all decided to stay.

The success of Infosys owes a lot to the attitude of the founders. Right from the first day, they made the interest of the company their top priority, setting a few ground rules, which each of them diligently followed. This attitude propelled Infosys to become the first IT company from India to be listed on NASDAQ.

Treating failure as a by-product of success and achievement, not letting it sap his spirit or slacken his morale, Murthy continued with his company in spite of the hurdles and hardships, making Infosys an IT giant.

Called the 'Father of Indian IT sector' by *Time* magazine, Murthy is a recipient of several awards, including the Padma Shri and Padma Vibhushan bestowed on him by the Indian government and Officier de la Legion d'Honneur (Officer of the Legion of Honor) by the Government of France. Murthy is not only an entrepreneur but also a philanthropist who believes in giving back to society.

31

PANKAJ ADVANI

Focus on the Moment

The reason Arjuna, the third Pandava brother, was considered the best archer in the world was his ability to focus on the situation in the present moment by turning off the other visual distractions, removing all the clutter from his mind and vision. He was the only one who could see the eye of the fish, unlike the other students of the famous teacher Drona. Like the sharp point of a needle, Arjuna pierced the eye of the fish, first with his single-minded focus and then with his arrow. It is this kind of undiluted focus that leads one to success and achievements.

Horses are made to wear blinkers or blinders for this very reason. These blinkers—small squares of leather or tack, sometimes even plastic cups—are attached to horses' hoods or bridles to block their sideways vision. Carriage and wagon-pulling horses are made to wear blinkers to prevent them from getting distracted or panicking by what they see behind the wagon. The purpose of the blinders is to cover the rear vision of the horse, thereby forcing it to look only ahead, thus keeping it on track.

People who achieve any modicum of success are masters at focusing, and their power of concentration is unbelievable.

India's ace snooker and billiards player Pankaj Advani has

mastered the art of focusing so well, winning for himself 24 world titles. It's not an unusual sight to see Advani, his eyes on the green baize, his fingers holding his cue stick, his concentration unwavering, tuning out the world, zoning out from his thoughts as he plots his next move or his next big break.

Born on 24 July 1985 in Pune, Advani achieved the rare feat, mother of all hat-tricks in English billiards, holding the World, Asian and Indian National Championship titles simultaneously in five different years—2005, 2008, 2012, 2017 and 2019. That's a testimony to his prowess and the power of his focus.

After having spent a few years in Kuwait, Advani's family settled down in Bangalore, with him joining Frank Anthony Public School. Advani was introduced to snooker by his elder brother Shree. The 10-year-old Advani latched on to his older brother, trailing his sibling to pool parlours where he played. Advani got so hooked to both billiards and snooker that for practice, he used a carrom board, marbles and chopsticks. The signs of focus, dedication and the desire to achieve his goal were obvious from a young age.

Within a year, 11-year-old Advani trumped his older brother in a small snooker tournament. Soon his proficiency came to the attention of Arvind Sarur, the former national snooker champion, who trained him. In 2000, Advani won his first Indian Junior Billiards Championship title, winning it again in 2001 and 2003, becoming the youngest national snooker champion in India.

Making his international debut at the Asian Billiards Championship 2002 in Bangalore, Advani stunned everyone by winning the World Amateur Snooker Champion title in 2003 and the IBSF World Billiards Championship in 2005 at Qawra, Malta.

This stickler for perfection has made winning a habit, never giving up until he is satisfied with the outcome of the game. This trait makes him India's most consistent and successful sportsperson. The mentally strong Advani has the ability to forget everything, from previous successes to failures, and just focus on the present moment. Even if he has played a bad shot, he doesn't let the ghost of that slip-up haunt him neither does he weaken emotionally; he once again refocuses on the game, giving the present moment his undivided attention and chalking up his wins.

When Advani was playing against the 18-year-old Chinese potting sensation Zhao Xintong, considered by many as a prodigy, in the IBSF World Snooker final in 2015 in Hurghada, Egypt, Advani, aware that the slightest slip-up could make him lose the game, never for a moment let his guard down. So watchful was Advani that even the slight fluttering of his opponent's eyelids wouldn't have gone unnoticed. Advani matched Xintong's fabulous shots with his superb return safeties, trying to frustrate his opponent into making errors. With unwavering focus, Advani worked his way to a 7-6 lead in the best-of-15 frame encounter. When Xintong fluffed a regulation pot, Advani was quick to catch that his opponent was upset at himself for that error. A good player not just plays at his best, but he also capitalizes on his opponent's weakness. A slight slackening from the opposite player is enough for him to race to the finish line. Advani knew that this was his chance to finish the match. Capitalizing on that momentary weakness of his opponent, Advani went on to complete a century break of 109, sealing the fate of the championship in his favour and winning 8-6.

Advani attributes his winning streak to the trophies he won in the start of his career, as these wins strengthened his mindset, instilling in him a self-belief that came in handy in his later games.

From the age of 18, when he won his first title in China in 2003, Advani's passion for the game and his hunger for victories remains as high as it was on the eve of his first final match. Born with nerves of steel, he has the ability to turn a pressure situation to his advantage.

In the final of the IBSF World Billiards Championship in Myanmar, on 15 September 2019, Advani was at his focused best, dominating the match from the start, giving his opponent Nay Thway Oo no chance at all. Fluent breaks helped his 6-2 win. Not for a single moment did Advani's concentration dip, and his unwavering focus helped him sail through effortlessly.

As billiards and snooker both require immense concentration, getting into the right zone by tuning out everything both externally and internally is important. Always trying to elevate his game, believing that success is more a state of mind, he repeatedly tells himself that he must play at his best.

Like wine, Advani has become better with age. With his deadly precision and faultless moves, Advani has become a champion at monopolizing the tables with his cue and flattening his opponents.

In recognition of his achievements, the Government of India has bestowed several awards upon him—the Arjuna Award, Major Dhyan Chand Khel Ratna Award, Padma Shri and the Padma Bhushan. Advani's achievements continue to inspire youngsters into picking up the cue stick.

32

P.C. SORCAR

Believe in Magic

Books transport us to a magical world, making us temporarily forget real life. When seven-year-old Alice, sitting with her sister near the riverbank, saw a white rabbit, nattily dressed and carrying a stopwatch, run past her as though he was in a hurry to reach somewhere, she followed it, tumbling down a rabbit hole into what turned out to be a wonderland in Lewis Carroll's book *Alice in Wonderland*, taking with her thousands of readers. It wasn't just Alice meeting the strange creatures, it was the readers too. That's the power of a magical place; it transports one instantly to a make-believe world, where one temporarily forgets real life, immersing themselves in the magic of the story the author has woven, getting absorbed in the strange world.

When the protagonist of J.K. Rowling's *Harry Potter* series of books, the bespectacled boy with the lightning-shaped scar on his forehead, received the owl from Hogwarts School of Witchcraft and Wizardry, announcing his admission into the school, millions of readers followed Harry through platform 9¾ to board the Hogwarts Express, taking them to Hogwarts. And after that the readers continued to board the same train every year, immersing themselves in the world of witches and wizards, where magic throbbed everywhere and anything was possible. Rowling's fantasy world so absorbed the readers, making them reluctant to leave it because for the duration of their reading, they believed in the world of wizards and witches.

Both Carroll and Rowling channelled the magic of their words to take generations of readers into their books.

Protul Chandra Sorcar or P.C. Sorcar, as he was known on stage, was a magician and illusionist and also a big believer in the power of magic to entertain, to transport his audience from the humdrum routine of their lives to a make-believe world where anything was possible.

India's culture and traditions have always fascinated the West, but they also had a preconceived notion about India, associating it with elephants, half-naked and meditating sadhus, and redolent maharajas reclining on their ornamental thrones, the great Indian rope trick and snake charmers. And then there were some who associated Indian magic with tantric and other occult activities. Sorcar, with his array of magic tricks, not only delighted his audiences, he also changed the way Indian magic was perceived by the West.

Born on 23 February 1913 into a Bengali family in Ashekpur village in Tangail district of East Bengal (now Bangladesh), Sorcar, right from childhood, was in love with magic more than mathematics, even as he displayed a good proficiency in the latter in school. While studying in Shibnath High School, Sorcar would stun his classmates with his magic tricks, illusions and sleight of hand, sometimes using their stationery as his objects. It wasn't unusual to see boys huddled around him, clamouring for more tricks.

Coming from a humble background, Sorcar knew that magic wasn't a financially lucrative profession. Nevertheless, he shifted to Calcutta to further his career. In Calcutta, he studied under Ganapati Chakraborty, a magician considered the pioneer of modern magic in India. Sorcar started performing in the clubs and theatres in Calcutta while he was still in his teens.

Post his BA from Ananda Mohan College in 1933, Sorcar turned to magic full-time, starting his brand of magic or illusion called Indrajaal (meaning, illusion in Sanskrit). He also changed the spelling of his surname from Sarkar to Sorcar.

Sorcar then went on an image-building spree; he became his own best salesman, calling himself the world's greatest magician. This was also a sign of his immense confidence in his abilities. He started an aggressive promotion campaign—large billboards announced his shows, business cards with his name and flyers promoting his magic shows were dished out to everyone.

Sorcar's first international performance was in Chicago in 1950 at the Sherman Hotel's conference hall, at the joint invitation of International Brotherhood of Magicians and the Society of American Magicians. Sorcar weaved his magic spell over the audience. He held packed shows all over the world—US, Europe, Japan, China, Russia, Australia and many other countries. The venues ranged from concert halls, theatres to stadiums. Sorcar not just found a place for himself on the global magic stage mostly dominated by European magicians, but he also earned full-page reviews and articles in popular newspapers abroad.

A stylish magician, Sorcar's shows were extravagant in their opulence, displaying India's grandeur to the world. Dressed in rich sherwanis and silk pants, a pearl necklace around his neck, a turban with a brooch on his head, the stage sometimes resembling the Taj Mahal, the backdrop painted in rich colours, showing trumpeting elephants. This was India at its exotic best. Sauntering to the stage, Sorcar would draw a mandala on the stage, lighting a lamp before a portrait of Goddess Durga, invoking Her blessings.

His retinue of assistants, both male and female, dressed in exotic clothes, helped him bring to life the magic that made people's body hum with happiness and delight.

One of Sorcar's popular tricks was called 'Water of India', in which he took a big jug, filled it up with water and then poured out the water in front of the audience. To verify that all the water was drained from the jug, Sorcar would invite a member of the audience to ascertain that the jug was empty. After the verification, Sorcar would say an incantation, then chant 'Water of India', as though he was summoning the water, and when he tilted the jug, water gushed out, driving the audience wild.

Once, at the Imperial Restaurant in Calcutta, Sorcar displayed his magic talent before Fazlul Huq, the chief minister of undivided Bengal. Sorcar requested Huq to write something on a piece of paper and then asked some of Huq's ministers to sign that paper. When Sorcar showed the paper, it revealed the ministers' signatures, announcing their resignations, much to everyone's shock; the paper also showed Sorcar's appointment as the new chief minister.

Sorcar, the Padma Shri awardee, was feted with several honours—The Sphinx Award, German Goldbar and the Dutch Tricks Prize, to name a few. Married to Basanti Devi, Sorcar's legacy was carried forward by two of his children, P.C. Sorcar Jr and P.C. Sorcar Young.

Sorcar died of a heart attack on 6 January 1971 during a performance in Asahikawa, Japan, collapsing while leaving the stage. The showman died while doing what he loved the most—transporting his viewers to a world of magic.

33

RAJINIKANTH

Find Your Own Unique Style

*I*t's believed that successful people don't do different things, they do things differently. Successful people add their unique touch to everything they do, putting the stamp of their individuality on the activities they undertake, leaving their distinctive mark on the world. And this is what differentiates them from the rest of the tribe. Over time, this trait becomes their hallmark and their ticket to success.

To find one's unique style, one first needs to realize what are one's assets and flaws. The second step is to capitalize on the assets by focusing on them and making it one's unique selling proposition.

If we want to see individuality, we just have to look at our kitchen, more specifically the spices lining its shelves. Tantalizing our taste buds, these spices are the perfect example of uniqueness. Each and every spice has a distinct flavour, look and taste, and these spices have not only earned their place in our cuisines, they also go on to decide how a dish will look, taste and smell, courtesy of the special identity of each of these spices. From the tiniest spice, the carom seeds to cloves, strings of saffron, the fragrant cardamom, sticks of cinnamon and the large bay leaves, they are all known for their strong personality.

All the trees and flowers in nature highlight their special quality too. The petals of the rose, unfurling like a secret, the sunflower turning towards the sun, the lotus floating in the breeze in the midst of a muddy lake.

Similarly, many people not only discover their uniqueness but also channel it in such a way that it becomes their signature style. It not only defines them, but they own that style, carving a niche for themselves in their chosen profession.

Luckily for cinema lovers, Shivaji Rao Gaekwad channelled his uniqueness to mesmerize Tamil cinema lovers, becoming the highest-grossing actor in the history of Tamil cinema—we are talking about none other than the superstar Rajinikanth.

Born on 12 December 1950 into a Marathi family in Bangalore, he was named Shivaji Rao Gaekwad after the Maratha king Shivaji, who his police constable father, Ramoji Rao Gaekwad, and his homemaker mother admired.

The youngest of four siblings, Rajinikanth studied at the Gavipuram Government Kannada Model Primary School in Bangalore. In childhood, mischief, cricket, football and basketball kept him busy. When his brother enrolled him in the Ramakrishna Math to learn the Vedas and history, Rajinikanth's interest in both spirituality and acting awakened. Rajinikanth acted for the first time at the age of six when he played the role of Ekalavya's friend from the epic Mahabharata at the Ramakrishna Math. He continued acting in plays even in his new school, the Acharya Pathasala Public School.

After completing his schooling, Rajinikanth did several odd jobs before joining the Bangalore Transport Service (BTS) as a bus conductor. He continued acting in Kannada plays on the side. To hone his acting skills, he joined the Madras Film Institute in 1973 to do a diploma. Here, he met the Tamil film director

K. Balachander. Sadly, at the first meeting, Rajinikanth wasn't able to impress Balachander with his imitation of Sivaji Ganesan's acting. Seeing a lot of potential in Rajinikanth, Balachander advised him to develop a style of his own and also learn Tamil.

Rajinikanth did both—he learnt Tamil and worked on developing a unique style. Herein lies the reason for the distinct and inimitable style differentiating Rajinikanth from other actors. At their next meeting, Balachander was impressed with the mannerisms Rajinikanth had developed and the acting skills he had worked on. He cast him in his film *Apoorva Raagangal* in 1975, albeit in a small role, but Rajinikanth managed to impress the audience with his performance.

Rajinikanth's first major role was in Balachander's Telugu film *Anthuleni Katha* in 1976. In the same year, Balachander cast him in his Tamil film *Moondru Mudichu*. The audience went crazy with Rajinikanth's mannerisms in the film. His signature style of flipping the cigarette and his dialogue delivery drove the audiences wild, so much so that they thronged the cinema houses repeatedly to see him on the big screen. Rajinikanth the star had arrived.

Rajinikanth played to the gallery, choosing his scripts carefully, playing larger-than-life roles, ensuring that his character appealed to the masses and that they could identify with it. He continued to work on developing his unique style. Opening a gate with his leg while smoking a cigar, delivering the punchlines in a stylish way, he developed his trademark style of walking and endearing expressions—with each move, he made a place for himself in the audiences' heart. His gravity-defying stunts made the audiences' jaws drop.

Mullum Malarum and *Aval Appadithan* in 1978 established Rajinikanth's acting credentials; by now, he had wooed the critics too with his talent. Rajinikanth's double role in the action thriller *Billa* in 1980 not only became his biggest commercial success, it also put him firmly on the throne of an action hero.

By the time the 1990s rolled in, Rajinikanth had established himself as a commercial star giving hit films one after another. His success reached humungous heights when *Baashha* (1995) released. The role of a crime boss in *Baashha* made his fan following explode through the roof. After that, a godlike status trailed him in Tamil Nadu. When he delivered the famous dialogue from *Baashha*, 'Naan oru thadava sonna nooru thadava sonna maadiri (If I say it once, then I've said it a hundred times),' it became a rage. People of all ages started repeating this dialogue.

Destiny had more fame in store for Rajinikanth. K.S. Ravikumar's film *Muthu* (1995) was dubbed in Japanese, resulting in a massive fan following for Rajinikanth in Japan. Each successful film strengthened his superstar status. At one point in time, Rajinikanth became the highest-paid actor in Asia after Jackie Chan. His double role of a scientist and an andro-humanoid robot in the 2010 science-fiction film *Enthiran* and its 2018 sequel *2.0* became super-duper hits.

In his long career, Rajinikanth has essayed a wide variety of roles, winning six Tamil Nadu State Film Awards in the Best Actor category, two Special Awards for Best Actor and a Filmfare Award for Best Tamil Actor. The Padma Bhushan and Padma Vibhushan awardee also received the Chevalier Sivaji Ganesan Award for Excellence in Indian Cinema, the Dadasaheb Phalke Award and several other awards.

Thalaivaa (meaning, leader), as Rajinikanth is often called, has carved a special place in the hearts of generations of fans. It isn't unusual to see three generations of a family eagerly thronging theatres to watch their favourite superstar's latest release.

34

R.K. LAXMAN

Look for the Unusual in the Usual

Award-winning photo journalists or professional photographers have that special trait of looking for the unusual in the usual. It may be a crowded marketplace, but their camera would have zoomed in to capture the image of a small girl licking an ice lolly. A group of septuagenarians in a park, and their lens would have focused on the gnarled hands of two senior citizens clasped together in an act of seeking comfort and warmth. A bunch of noisy children running around in a playground, but the focus of their camera would be two children, one bending down to tie the other's shoelaces.

A thick canopy of trees, but the subject of the camera's lens is a tiny yellow bird perched on one of the branches. A verdant field, lush with rainbow-hued flowers, and the camera would zoom in to capture the image of a bee sucking nectar from a flower. A photo of a large eagle, its wings spread wide, with a glorious sunset in the background. A lush garden wet with rain, but the camera goes in for a close-up of a large leaf, with a single drop of water sparkling in the sunshine like a pearl. What sets all these photos apart from other photographs carrying similar visages is the ability to look for the unusual in the usual, which we often miss in our monotonous lives.

Luckily, Rasipuram Krishnaswami Iyer Laxman had the ability and the perceptive eye to look for the unusual in the usual. Who are we talking of? It's R.K. Laxman, India's leading cartoonist, illustrator and humourist.

Born on 24 October 1921 in Mysore into a Vaishnavite Vadama Brahmin family, Laxman was the youngest of eight children. With Laxman's father being the headmaster in a school, it was obvious that Laxman was surrounded by books and magazines while growing up. As a child, even before he learnt to read, he would flip through the pages of magazines—*The Strand*, *Punch*, *Bystander*, *Wide World* and *Tit-Bits*—scattered around his house, engrossed in the illustrations.

Needless to say, this fascination with illustrations not just exposed him to myriad styles but also kick-started his own love affair with drawing. Laxman started sketching from a young age. Everything he saw around the house—cows, crows, lizards, birds, leaves and dry twigs—were the subject of his initial doodles. His father and teachers weren't spared, neither were the house staff. It wasn't unusual to see Laxman make his drawings and caricatures on the walls, floors and the doors of his house, using them as his canvas. His drawings displayed his penchant for comedy.

The young Laxman was fascinated with the British cartoonist Sir David Low's illustrations in *The Hindu* newspaper. Low's style became one of Laxman's earliest influences.

Laxman started taking his drawing more seriously when his schoolteacher praised his sketch of a peepul leaf. That was the moment when the idea that he could illustrate for a living was cemented in Laxman's head.

Laxman's carefree childhood received a rude jolt when his father had a paralytic stroke, dying a year later. But the family elders ensured that Laxman's schooling continued uninterrupted. After completing his school, Laxman, keen on studying at

Sir J.J. School of Art, sent his application. Much to his dismay, the dean of the school rejected his admission, giving the reason that he found Laxman's drawings lacking in the kind of talent students of the institute must have. Though disappointed, Laxman moved to his next plan, completing his Bachelor of Arts from the Maharaja's College of Mysore.

While studying in college, he illustrated his older brother R.K. Narayan's stories published in *The Hindu*. He also started working as a part-time cartoonist for local newspapers and magazines. His first full-time job as a political cartoonist for *The Free Press Journal* in Bombay sharpened his creativity, which came in handy when he joined *The Times of India*, Bombay, in 1951, creating a daily comic strip called *You Said It*, appearing on the front page.

You Said It, a humorous comic strip with the Common Man as the protagonist, showcased the daily dilemmas and problems of every Indian. It gave an outlet to the plight of Indians, striking an instant connection with the readers. They considered the Common Man their cartoon avatar, vocalizing their thoughts and feelings.

With the cartoon strip becoming popular pan-India, it was the biggest turning point in Laxman's career. The pocket-sized cartoon featuring a bespectacled Common Man, wearing a checked coat over a plain white dhoti, his balding pate and tufts of white hair growing on the sides of his head, was not just witnessing the making of the democracy in India, he was also viewing it from the perspective of a common man.

Laxman had an eye for seeing the usual and presenting it in an unusual way. The cartoon strip *Incredible India*, showing the Common Man stripped to his underwear, reclining on a bed of needles or pins, laughing at the motley crowd of tourists clicking his picture, points to the slew of problems a common man faces in his daily life, yet he finds something to smile about.

Another cartoon with the Common Man raising his hands at the petrol station with the dispenser pointed like a gun at him was Laxman's commentary on the rising fuel price and its effect on the citizens.

Gentle humour was Laxman's forte, and his cartoons amply demonstrated his penchant for it, such as the cartoon with the Common Man and his friend staring at the billboard with the picture of a smiling man, with a television set beside him, the Common Man telling his friend, 'Remarkable chap, promotes TV sets, bath soaps, soft drinks, hotels, etc., besides he is a cricket champion!'

Most of Laxman's cartoons brought a smile on the readers' faces, with his gentle irony matching what was running in their mind. The cartoon of the budget of 1997–98, with the frazzled Common Man being marched by the prime minister on one side and the finance minister carrying the banner of prosperity on the other side, the Opposition standing at a distance saying that he has been kidnapped and we must rescue him is yet another testimony of Laxman's genius.

Feted with the Padma Bhushan, Padma Vibhushan, Ramon Magsaysay Award and the Rajyotsava Award from the Government of Karnataka, Laxman was largely a self-taught artist whose pen brought to life the different situations ordinary citizens found themselves in, albeit in a humorous way.

Laxman died on 26 January 2015 in Pune, leaving a void in the heart of his admirers who had found solace in his cartoon strip and a kindred soul in his Common Man.

35

R.K. NARAYAN

Find Inspiration Everywhere

Inspiration, like the air we breathe, is everywhere, and artists of all kind find this inspiration to create their masterpieces. Looking out of the window, seeing the rain pattering down, a musician gets the inspiration for his melody in the sound of the rain; the fire crackling in the fireplace inspires his background score; the wind howling through the trees becomes the music for his next song; and the cacophony of the traffic as well as the screech of an eagle find their way into his compositions.

Standing on a terrace, watching a tree, its brown leaves scattered on the ground, a bird perched on one of its bare branches, a poet finds inspiration for his prize-winning poem. A husband and wife bickering while walking on the road makes its way to a writer's story or an article in the newspaper.

The colours of nature, the glorious sunset with its pink and orange streaks, the mellow sunrise, the bright flowers swaying in the breeze, a bird, its wings spread, flying against the backdrop of a glowing sun, finds its representation in a painting. The velvety petal of a red rose triggers a haiku, as does a dew drop trickling down a leaf and the gleaming edge of a knife.

Dutch painter Vincent van Gogh found the subject for one of his paintings in his doctor, with whom he was spending some time as a part of his treatment. *Portrait of Dr Gachet* was the result. For Norwegian painter Edvard Munch, a stroll with friends turned inspirational when he glanced at the red-streaked sky, accompanied by a creaking sound, as though the city was making the noise. The setting resulted in his painting titled *The Scream*.

If Rasipuram Krishnaswami Iyer Narayanaswami or R.K. Narayan, as he is better known, hadn't found inspiration everywhere, making what he saw the theme of his books, weaving brilliant stories around it, then India would have been deprived of one of its all-time favourite books—*Swami and Friends*.

Born on 10 October 1906 in Madras into a Vaishnavite Vadama Brahmin family, from childhood, Narayan and his seven siblings were surrounded by books, courtesy of their school headmaster father.

Due to his father's transfers, Narayan spent a large chunk of his childhood with his maternal grandmother. A formidable lady, she was instrumental in enhancing Narayan's skills and knowledge in many subjects, and these came in handy later in life when he wove his stories and etched his different characters. Narayan's father, with his penchant for grammar, which he inculcated in all his children, made them always speak grammatically correct English. As Narayan grew, this fondness for speaking perfect English enabled him to craft his impeccable sentences, building them into wonderful stories.

Narayan studied in several schools: Lutheran Mission School, C.R.C. High School as well as the Christian College High School in Madras. After Narayan's father was transferred to the Maharaja High School and Pre-University College in Mysore, the well-stocked school library turned Narayan into a voracious reader. He devoured books written by Charles Dickens, P.G. Wodehouse, Arthur Conan Doyle and Thomas Hardy at an alarming rate. Side by side, perhaps inspired by the great writers he read, he also started writing his own stories.

After completing his BA from Maharaja's College, Mysore, Narayan worked as a schoolteacher for a short while, but the pull of writing was strong; quitting his job, he turned towards writing full-time. While working on his novels, he also freelanced for English newspapers and magazines. Being a man of few needs, he managed on his meagre income—his first-year writing income was a paltry sum of nine rupees and 12 annas. Luckily for Narayan, his family and friends supported him in his career choice.

Narayan wrote his first novel, *Swaminathan and Tate,* in 1930, creating Malgudi, a small, fictional, stereotypical town in South India, ruled by superstitions and age-old traditions. The image of a railway station came up in Narayan's mind one day and the idea for Malgudi was born. This was followed by the name Malgudi, and finally the character of Swami appeared in Narayan's mind. Narayan combined the three to start his novel *Swaminathan and Tate*, adding many personal incidents from his childhood, making it a semi-autobiographical novel.

After the manuscript faced a slew of rejections from publishers, Narayan sent it to a friend in Oxford, who showed the manuscript to Graham Greene. Impressed with the story, Greene sent the book to his publishing house, where it was accepted. Greene became a mentor figure to Narayan. It was at Greene's suggestion that he shortened his name to R.K. Narayan and also titled the book as *Swami and Friends*. Published in 1935, the book's sale suffered, though it garnered good reviews.

For his next novel, *The Bachelor of Arts*, Narayan once again looked for inspiration nearby, using his college experiences, the rebellious adolescent phase that many youngsters go through before their transition into adulthood, as the leitmotif of the novel. Narayan's third novel, *The Dark Room*, was based on the trouble in marriages he saw around him.

For his novel *The English Teacher*, Narayan once again borrowed inspiration from his own life. His wife Rajam's death due to typhoid in 1939, leaving him with their three-year-old daughter Hema, found literary soulmates in the characters of Krishna and his wife Susila who died of typhoid, leaving behind their daughter Leela. The book was a fictionalized account of Narayan's bereavement, putting words to the emotions he underwent at his wife's death.

Everything he saw around him, especially the socially prevalent practices of those times, found its way into his stories. His books were a social commentary depicting the everyday life of characters in small towns, infused with gentle humour.

Narayan's experience of writing a journal found its literary soulmate in Mr Sampath, the character in *The Printer of Malgudi*. His daily journal writing became the inspiration for *My Dateless Diary*. Malgudi featured in many of his novels.

Winner of the Sahitya Akademi Award in 1958 for his novel *The Guide*, Narayan's characters made the readers visualize their next-door neighbours or the people living on their street. Narayan's writing was simple and earthy; his protagonists were ordinary people with many quirks, living humdrum lives, getting into spots, creating a bond with the readers. The Padma Bhushan and Padma Vibhushan awardee's writing career spanned 60 years.

Narayan died on 13 May 2001 in Chennai. To Narayan goes the credit for making the rest of the world take notice of Indian writing. Narayan's books were like a family treasure, passed from father to child, each generation finding delight in the stories and the characters.

36

RAMKINKAR BAIJ

First Learn the Rules, Then Break Them

'*L*earn the rules like a pro so you can break them like an artist,' said the Spanish painter Pablo Picasso.

Great painters and artists first diligently learn the rules of their art, absorbing all the finer nuances of their craft. Then, once they have perfectly understood their craft, perhaps subconsciously their minds begin to work on how to break all the rules by pushing the boundaries, innovating, improvising, blending different elements to create something new, infusing influences that enhance their art and pushing the edges to create new lines. Post their learning, the world becomes their oyster.

For great artists, the rules of their craft are like a piece of elastic, which they can bend at will. At times, they treat the rules like a lump of clay, moulding them with their talent until it forms new figures, which become the new rules that someone in the distant future will break with their creativity. Only by a perfect understanding of their craft can they experiment with it, turning whatever they have learnt on its head and displaying their talent and ingenuity.

For the maestros, learning technicalities of their craft is like studying in a box, with the tight lines holding them inside. For these artists, this boxed learning is claustrophobic. They are eager to break free of its shackles. The innovations they bring to their art is imbued with the jagged outlines of their rebellious streak, coloured with their independent thinking, shaped with their personal style and stamped with their strong individuality.

Ramkinkar Baij, sculptor and painter, was a perfect example of learning the rules, mastering it and then breaking it. A pioneer of modern Indian sculpture, Baij is known for his spontaneity in his work and he indeed was, to a large extent, guided by his instinct.

Born on 25 May 1906 in Bankura district of undivided Bengal into a Bengali family with little financial standing, Baij grew up amidst the local craftsmen and idol-makers. As they lived nearby, he often watched them create beautiful handicrafts and sculptures, and taking inspiration from them, the self-taught boy crafted small figures from clay. Baij's artistic talent wasn't dependent on easels and paints; he painted, improvising with whatever materials he could lay his hands on. In his teens, Baij painted portraits of Indian freedom fighters, inspired by their determination and fortitude. When the famous journalist Ramananda Chatterjee saw these political posters, seeing the potential in him, he advised Baij to join Kala Bhavan, Santiniketan, to hone his skills.

Baij joined Kala Bhavan in 1925, and under Rabindranath Tagore and Nandalal Bose's training, his artistic genius took shape. Though Baij learnt all the artistic rules, mastering them to perfection, he also broke them magnificently to create his individualistic and innovative style.

One day, Baij attended a session on clay modelling conducted by a visiting French sculptor. Though the session was short, it captivated his interest. Clay modelling soon became his passion. Baij started reading books on clay modelling in the Kala Bhavan library, learning about the western influences in sculpture, innovating with the techniques he read about until he came up with his unique style, called abstract modern sculptures.

Baij was a master of innovation. As plaster of Paris was too expensive, he used cement concrete casting in his sculptures, combining these with laterite pebbles he sourced from nearby regions. Baij's sculptures, in fact his entire art, was rooted in Indianness. For his oil paintings, he used Santhal wraps with packet colours, diluting these with linseed oil to get the texture he wanted. He innovated by drawing his figures on silk, using a shoe brush. Sometimes he painted on bed sheets, as canvases were expensive.

Baij disliked the statue-like style of sculpting. He believed that momentum created the tension in an artist's work. His personal philosophy that his sculptures should have the fluidity of movement, as though they were in motion, saw him craft several masterpieces. His sculpture *Santhal Family*, a tribal couple with two children and a dog, carrying their belongings, has an inexplicable energy and movement; it looks as though the tribal family is walking somewhere, and Baij has caught them mid-stride. Created in 1938–39, this sculpture is considered his magnum opus.

Another sculpture titled *Call of the Mill* depicts a couple of factory workers running towards the mill on hearing the siren, their child behind them. Again, this sculpture has the energy of movement. It looks as though the workers have been captured while running.

Baij always kept Rabindranath Tagore's teaching in mind: 'When you observe something, grab it like a tiger by the nape of the neck. And then, never look back.' When Baij took over the department of sculpture at Kala Bhavan, he often advised his students to go outdoors and sketch so that they could capture the spirit of their object in its environment.

Baij's creative genius is evident in his painting titled *Harvesting*, which depicts a group of men thrashing paddy in a field. The painting focuses on their arms and legs and not their slightly bent heads, as though Baij had captured them while they were thrashing the stacks of paddy.

The Santiniketan campus hosts several of Baij's sculptures, from the serene statue of Buddha sitting in the lotus posture to the 11-foot tall and graceful sculpture titled *Sujata*, made from lateritic granules, coarse lateritic earth and gravel, all blended with cement. Baij's concrete structures rising from the ground have a larger-than-life feel, suiting the outdoors locations they are a part of. Though cement was perfectly suitable for the intense heat and the heavy rains of West Bengal, it had a problem—it hardened extremely fast, making it difficult for the artist to shape his sculptures. This disadvantage wasn't present in sculptures made from wax or clay. Baij made each of his sculptures around metal armatures, then applied the paste in clumps, later chiselling out the excess, which resulted in a uniquely textured surface.

Baij's brush with fame came in the 1970s when the Government of India commissioned him to create two sculptures of a yaksha and yakshi for the Reserve Bank of India headquarters in New Delhi. Crafting these gigantic sculptures from stone sourced from Baijnath in Himachal Pradesh, the sculptures showcase Baij's mastery of his craft.

Baij died on 2 August 1980 in Calcutta. The Padma Bhushan awardee, largely self-taught, turned around the rules of sculpting and painting with his raw talent to craft masterpieces.

37

Ritu Kumar

Blend the Old with the New

Fashion is a perfect example of blending the old with the new. It's said that fashion is cyclic, the old returns time and again with a makeover, a new personality, a new identity, but deep down, at its core, it's the same.

Blending the old with the new is also a way to keep the old alive by giving it a contemporary twist to make it appealing to the current generation. The old favourite is infused with a new favourite until a fusion takes place, resulting in an offspring that's an amalgamation of both.

Fusion cuisine is an apt example of the blending of the old with the new. To keep the old food relevant, chefs present them in an innovative way: gajar halwa, the old favourite, is blended with the new favourite, momos, resulting in gajar halwa momos. Mysore pak and muffins are brought together in a funky combination called Mysore pak muffins. Kaju katli and fudge merge to form katli fudge. Take the old, which has less takers, give it a quirky twist and one has instantly chalked up the admirers and increased the fan following.

Baggy bell-bottoms become trendy flared pants, loose pyjamas take a detour and become palazzos for women. Dupattas shed the excess weight and length, becoming slimmer and sleeker stoles, sometimes becoming trendy scarves. The humble churidar takes the metro, alighting with a new persona called leggings. The old constantly undergoes a metamorphosis to appeal to the current generation.

Fashion designer Ritu Kumar successfully blended the old with the new to create elegant outfits, both coveted and cherished by women. Before Kumar's arrival on the fashion scene, women flocked to the neighbourhood darzi (tailor), their arms loaded with dress materials, perhaps a torn piece of magazine paper in their hands, hoping to copy some film star's designer wear.

Kumar was born on 11 November 1944 in Amritsar into a traditional family. She studied in Loreto Convent Tara Hall boarding school in Shimla. From Loreto, she joined Lady Irwin College, completing her degree. Neither in school nor in college did fashion designing figure in her life.

Kumar's fascination with textile and craft heritage was ignited when, at 20, she visited a family of block-makers. The ancient designs and weaves invoked in her a desire to revive them. She signed up for a course in art history in New York's Briarcliffe College. Post her return to India, Ritu married Shashi Kumar and shifted to Calcutta.

With a constant desire to further her knowledge of Indian art, fabrics, crafts and patterns, she studied museology at the Asutosh Museum of Indian Art, Calcutta University. Both these courses, art history and museology, exposed Kumar to past trends, to the different art forms and heritages lost in the annals of history, making her think of ways she could bring them back into usage.

Kumar set up her fashion business in a village near Calcutta where traditional craftsmen lived, with just two small tables and four hand-block printers. The late 1960s was a time when designer wear hadn't entered popular domain, and boutique culture and haute couture were new concepts. She started her first store, Ritu's

Boutique, on Calcutta's Wellesley Street (now Rafi Ahmad Kidwai Street) in 1968, with bridalwear and evening clothes.

Kumar considers textiles a true reflection of a country's culture and tradition. To preserve this culture, she revived the textiles, weaves and printing styles on the verge of fading out, becoming a saviour of the kaarigars who were on the brink of becoming extinct. She used zardozi, the intricate embroidery in gold and silver threads, in wedding saris and lehangas to create masterpieces worn by brides on their wedding day. Kashida, the Kashmiri embroidery, which used thick-coloured threads to create stunning patterns, found itself in many salwar-kurtas and kaftans designed by Kumar. She made chikankari, the traditional embroidery of Lucknow, a rage, a must-have for every woman. She kept the kaarigars and spinners busy, churning out designs after designs.

Bandhani, kalamkari and other traditional dyeing and printing techniques, wearing their Indian heart on their designer sleeves, gave ethnic wear a new appeal. With a penchant for natural fabrics, Kumar based her new collections on them, giving a contemporary twist to her designs by way of innovative cuts, style and silhouettes, winning thousands of fans all over the world.

Soon, Kumar became one of the most sought-after designer brands in India. The credit for this lies with her for evolving a style that mirrored the ancient traditions of India, blending it with contemporary elements to craft elegant outfits that stood the test of time, each staking its rightful claim at being called an heirloom. Women dreamt of owning outfits designed by Kumar, and when they managed to buy that much-desired dress, they not just cherished it, but it held a pride of place in their wardrobes. Her clothes were a fusion of the traditional and the trendy. Though later she introduced western elements into her designs, her clothes have more often walked on the traditional path.

Kumar slowly ventured into the international market, opening branches in Paris, London and New York, places considered the fashion capitals of the world. It wasn't easy for an Indian woman to break into these high-end fashion houses and department stores. But Kumar managed to do it with her customary ease.

Keeping the heart and soul of her stores close to the Indian tradition, Kumar's boutiques started displaying her stylish western garments, which were based on Indian styles, appealing to women across ages and continents. There were dhoti pants coupled with kurtas with Indian motifs and embroideries, pre-draped sarees, kurta dresses in dark geometric prints, crinkled skirts in bold colours, paired with kurtas in pastels flaunting delicate mirror work and kaftan tops with traditional embroideries, for those wanting an Indo-western look. Kumar gave chanderi and jute fabrics new personas. Local fabrics underwent cuts and embraced motifs that lured the younger generation into her stores.

Kumar, a Padma Shri awardee, was also felicitated with the Chevalier des Arts et des Lettres (Knight of the Order of Arts and Letters) by the Government of France. Her designs have been worn by royalty to leading actresses, from brides to working professionals, from grandmothers to granddaughters.

Kumar's strength of a deep knowledge of textiles and how to use it effectively to maximize its appeal, coupled with her creativity, points to her sartorial genius, making her the rightful claimant to the title of 'prima donna of the Indian fashion industry'.

38

RUKMINI DEVI ARUNDALE

Be a Game Changer

Humanity has seen many game changers—events, inventions, ideas and discoveries that created a paradigm shift in the way certain things were seen, completely transforming the way certain things were done, impacting the entire society and reviving industries.

The telephone was a game changer. After Graham Bell's invention, communication was transformed completely. Letter-writing became passé; speaking on the telephone was faster and less cumbersome. When smartphones burst into the global scene, they took off from where the telephone had stopped. The television was another game changer, completely turning the ball of entertainment on its head.

In 1912 when Henry Ford's automobile the Model T Roadster arrived, it became a huge game changer for the automobile industry, resulting in the mass production of affordable cars that middle-class Americans could easily buy. This car had a huge impact on the economy, since it made it possible for people to travel long distances for work.

When the Zenith Flash-Matic TV remote was introduced in 1955, it was the first wireless TV remote using the technology of flashing lights to switch the TV sets on and off, also facilitating volume control. A game changer, it had an impact on the way people viewed television. Several years later, when the Zenith Space Command, a remote that used ultrasonic waves for channel surfing, arrived, it saw the birth of couch potatoes. It was succeeded in the 1980s by the infrared remote, forcing TV broadcasters to improve the quality of their shows and introduce more channels, as viewers now had the advantage of changing channels at the press of a button.

Personal computers, launched in August 1981 by IBM, were game changers, making computers business tools. Sliced bread was a game changer for the food industry, changing the way people ate their breakfast.

Rukmini Devi Arundale (nee Shashtri) was a game changer for the Indian classical dance form. She was instrumental in revitalizing Bharatanatyam and bringing it under the global spotlight. In fact, Bharatanatyam owes its current name to Arundale and her dance guru E. Krishna Iyer. Earlier it was called Sadhir.

Born on 29 February 1904 in Madurai into a Brahmin family, Arundale's father, Neelakanta Shastri, was an engineer with the public works department and a scholar, and her mother, Seshammal, a music aficionado. Because of her father's transferrable job, the family moved frequently from place to place. As her father was deeply influenced by the Theosophical Society of Dr Annie Besant, Arundale and her seven siblings were exposed to culture, art, music, dance and theatre from a young age. These influences shaped her personality and mindset, imbuing in her a love for music and dance. After retirement, her father settled down close to the Theosophical Society's headquarters in Madras.

As the British theosophist Dr George Arundale, a close friend of Besant, often dropped in at the Theosophical Society headquarters, he frequently bumped into Rukmini. The two fell in love, and their marriage in 1920 shocked the traditional society of Madras, steeped as it was in its conservative attitude.

After her marriage, Arundale travelled the world with her husband for many years. In 1928, when the famous Russian ballerina Anna Pavlova visited Bombay, Arundale and her husband, with their love for the performing arts, went to watch her performance.

Later, serendipity played a big role when the Arundale couple and Pavlova ended up travelling to Australia on the same ship. Not only did Arundale strike a friendship with Pavlova, it also resulted in her learning the western classical dance from one of the dancers of Pavlova's troupe. Seeing Arundale's fascination and passion for dance, Pavlova sowed the seeds for revivalism of the dance form in Arundale's mind by suggesting that she should revive the hitherto glorious traditional Indian dance forms.

This set the wheels in Arundale's mind in motion, but her real association with Bharatanatyam started much later. After her return to Madras in 1933, while attending the Annual Conference of the Madras Music Academy, Arundale saw a Sadhir dance performance. Enchanted with it, she started learning the dance form from Mylapore Gowri Amma, a famous dance teacher. Arundale further honed her dance skills by undergoing training from two stalwarts: E. Krishna Iyer and Pandanallur Meenakshi Sundaram Pillai. Two years later, at the Diamond Jubilee Convention of the Theosophical Society, Arundale gave her first public performance.

Over the years, Arundale gave Sadhir a makeover. Due to its association with temple dancers called the devadasis, Sadhir had an aura of eroticism attached to it. The extra sringar adopted by the temple dancers, both in make-up and gestures, was considered erotic by most of society, especially the elite class, who looked down upon it.

Arundale changed the very face of the dance form by introducing many elements into it, lifting it from the miasma of vulgarity. The first thing Arundale did was to transform these dance performances into elaborate dance dramas, depicting scenes from different episodes of the epics. She got eminent scholars and famous classical musicians to write the dance-drama scripts. With these scripts, Arundale produced elaborate dance dramas based on the epics: *Sita Swayamvaram, Gita Govindam, Sri Rama Vanagamanam, Paduka Pattabhishekam, Sabari Moksham* and *Usha Parinayam*.

Arundale got the stage designed in an aesthetic way; the addition of light infused the dance dramas with an enchanting quality, literally brushing away the curtain of darkness clinging to it. Not content with that, Arundale introduced musical instruments, with the violin especially enhancing the dance dramas. The dancers were fitted with elegant clothes and jewellery inspired by the temple sculptures of queens in their regalia. All these elements gave the dance an element of purity, which was missing earlier, making it appealing to the upper castes. Arundale transformed Sadhir into the polished Bharatanatyam, elevating it into a dance form with elements of spirituality and divine sublimity, wowing the elite and the Brahmins to such an extent that they allowed their daughters to learn Bharatanatyam.

Few years later, Arundale and her husband established Kalakshetra in Madras, a music and dance academy that kept the ancient gurukul system heritage alive, further popularizing Bharatanatyam, making it accessible to eager students.

By adding music, dance and story to the dance dramas, Arundale severed the umbilical cord of its association with devadasis, giving India and the world a dance form much admired. Arundale, a recipient of the Padma Bhushan, Sangeet Natak Akademi Award and Kalidas Samman by the Government of Madhya Pradesh, died on 24 February 1986 in Madras, leaving behind a rich legacy that is a hard act to follow, changing the rules of the game along the way.

39

SALIM ALI

Retain Your Curiosity and Your Keenness to Learn

A small child is the best example of retaining one's curiosity and the keenness to learn. The never-ending questions children ask, often mentally taxing their parents, reflects a trait that has its basis in their perpetual curiosity to know more about everything in life. This urge to learn more makes them blossom with knowledge as they grow older.

Only if we learn, can we grow; only if we soak in knowledge, can we bloom in understanding. If not for the innate curiosity of scientists, the world would have been devoid of many of its discoveries and inventions. This childlike trait of curiosity, always interested in the hows and the whys, obsessed with learning and furthering their knowledge, gives scientists the special ability to discover, invent and create things. Luckily for the rest of society, inventors are people blessed with an insatiable and unstoppable curiosity; their quest for knowledge is the most constant thing in their lives. Even after they have invented something, they are forever trying to perfect and improve that invention.

An example of perpetual curiosity is American inventor Beulah Louise Henry. When Henry was 25, she received her first patent for an ice-cream freezer in 1912. She went on to earn 49 more patents till the 1970s. She forged ahead to invent toys, household appliances and even industrial devices. She was not just America's leading female inventor, she also earned the nickname Lady Edison. Her logic was 'I invent because I cannot help it'. Henry was bitten by the twin bugs of curiosity and inventiveness, accompanied by the keenness to learn more and more in life.

India's ornithologists owe a great debt to the keenness and curiosity of Salim Moizuddin Abdul Ali or Salim Ali, one of the greatest ornithologists and naturalists India has seen. Known as the Birdman of India, Ali was one of the first few scientists to do systematic bird surveys, both in India and abroad. The development of the field of ornithology in India is based on Ali's extensive research work, which became the foundation stone for later ornithologists to build their work.

Born on 12 November 1896 in Bombay in a Sulaimani Bohra Muslim family, Ali was the youngest of nine children. Ali lost his father when he was a year old, and two years later, he was bereaved once again when his mother died. Ali and his siblings were brought up by their maternal uncle, Amiruddin Tyabji, and aunt Hamida Begum.

At a young age, Ali displayed an interest in reading books on hunting, and shooting became his new fascination. This fondness for hunting enabled him to get a toy airgun. When Ali was 10, he shot down a bird with his toy airgun. When he inspected the bird, he realized that though it looked like the common house sparrow, what differentiated it from the sparrow was the yellowish streak on its throat. Bitten by the bug of curiosity and with a keenness to know more about the bird, he showed it to his uncle. Unable to satisfy his nephew's curiosity, his uncle took him to W.S. Millard, the secretary of the Bombay Natural History Society (BNHS), where he was a member. Millard, with his extensive knowledge of birds, identified it as a yellow-throated sparrow, and he also showed Ali the stuffed collection of birds in BNHS. Seeing the young boy's eagerness to learn more about the avians, Millard gave him several books about birds. Returning home, Ali started reading the books. They fuelled the young boy's interest, making him start recording his bird sightings and observations in his diary. The diary writing resulted in Ali spending hours observing birds, especially the mating patterns of hen sparrows. One day, he saw a pair of sparrows. After he shot down the male sparrow, Ali sat down to watch, noticing that the female sparrow soon replaced her dead partner with another male sparrow. Ali jotted down this observation in his diary.

This was the turning point in Ali's life and the reason for his lifelong keenness to observe birds and learn more about them. Ali did his primary schooling from Zenana Bible and Medical Mission Girls High School. After his first year at St. Xavier's College, Bombay, Ali left for Burma (now Myanmar) to help his brother in the family's tungsten mining and timber business, but he spent most of his time birdwatching, honing his skills as a naturalist in Burma.

After returning to India in 1917, Ali attended morning classes in commercial law and accountancy from Davar's College of Commerce and evening classes in zoology from St. Xavier's College. Around the same time, he married Tehmina Begum.

Ali worked at the BNHS for a short period, taking visitors on guided tours of the museum. Alongside, he conducted bird research at his residence.

To learn more about birds, Ali left for Germany in 1928 to study under Dr Erwin Stresemann, a world-famous ornithologist in Berlin's Natural History Museum. When he returned to India in 1930, as his post at the museum had been removed, he shifted to his wife's house in Kihim, a small village in coastal Mumbai, making the most of the quiet place to study the baya weaver bird and its mating pattern. In the same year, he published a research paper discussing the nature of the weaver bird and its activities. It earned him acclaim, establishing his name in the field of ornithology.

Interested in studying birds in their natural environment, Ali travelled from place to place, conducting bird surveys, making detailed observations, which became the basis of his books. *The Book of Indian Birds* published in 1941, discussing the different kinds of Indian birds and their habitats, became a popular reference book for bird-lovers and ornithologists. Ali collaborated with S. Dillon Ripley, a world-famous ornithologist for the 10-volume *Handbook of the Birds of India and Pakistan*. A laborious project, it was a result of 10 years of research, describing the birds of the subcontinent, their appearance, behaviour, habitats, breeding habits and migratory patterns.

Passionate about protecting nature, Ali was instrumental in setting up the Bharatpur Bird Sanctuary (Keoladeo National Park). Without any formal training in the subject, Ali became a famous ornithologist. Carrying his diary and pen everywhere, he constantly jotted down his bird observations. Feted with the Padma Bhushan and the Padma Vibushan, Ali became the first non-British citizen to receive the Gold Medal of the British Ornithologists' Union, and many other honours.

Ali died on 20 June 1987. His curiosity and keenness to learn more about birds followed him throughout his life, elevating him to the realm of greatness in the field of ornithology.

40

SAM MANEKSHAW

Have the Courage of Your Convictions

Not many people have the courage of their convictions to follow through with the decision they have made or complete the task they have undertaken. More often than not this requires one to be a braveheart, shoving aside everything, especially the fears, to rise to the occasion, without a thought for their personal safety.

When armed terrorists lay siege to a building, holding a group of human hostages, police personnel or commandos entering the building don't know from which direction a bullet will come hurtling towards them or which corner holds a bomb. Yet, they put their lives at risk, egged on by the courage of their convictions to save human lives. This conviction tugs at their heart, giving them the guts to surge ahead, irrespective of the outcome. So is the case when a fireman plunges into a burning building to save a trapped mother and child—other than the protective gear, he also dons the cape of courage.

The policemen and the firemen answer the call of their conscience. Once they are convinced that their action would save lives, they summon the courage to go ahead with their plan. Having the courage of one's convictions gives people the confidence to do what they believe is the right thing, even when other people dissuade them from it.

Field Marshal Sam Hormusji Framji Jamshedji Manekshaw or Sam Manekshaw, as he is popularly known, has always been a man who had the courage of his convictions.

Born on 3 April 1914 in Amritsar, Punjab, into a Parsi family, Manekshaw's father, Hormusji, was a doctor and his mother, Hilla, a homemaker. Manekshaw was the naughtiest of Hormusji and Hilla's six children, always prone to mischief. The spirited boy did his schooling first in Amritsar, then in Sherwood College, Nainital, for his Junior Cambridge Certificate. After completing his Senior Cambridge with distinction, Manekshaw wanted to follow in his father's footsteps and study medicine in London.

His father refused, as he was already funding his older sons to go to London for their engineering course and he didn't have money for one more son. He also felt that the 17-year-old Manekshaw was too young to go to London. A disappointed Manekshaw joined the Hindu Sabha College, graduating with a science degree in 1932.

When Manekshaw came across a notice of the Indian Military Academy's three-year training course for officers in the army, seeing it as a perfect chance to rebel against his father for not sending him to London, he appeared for the entrance exam in Delhi and was subsequently selected. On 1 October 1932, Manekshaw and 39 other cadets started their training; the first batch was called the Pioneers.

Sometime during his training, Manekshaw developed the courage of his convictions, and what started as an act of rebellion became his true calling in life, the voice of his soul. Manekshaw, along with 22 cadets, successfully completed the course and were commissioned as second lieutenants into the British regiment on 1 February 1935. At that time, it was mandatory for newly commissioned Indian officers to serve in the British regiment before joining an Indian unit of the army.

Manekshaw's first posting was in Lahore in the 2nd Battalion, Royal Scots; then he moved to Burma, joining the 4th Battalion of the 12th Frontier Force Regiment. In the 1942 Burma Campaign, Manekshaw, now a captain, led his troops against the Imperial Japanese Army by mounting a successful counter-attack around the Pagoda Hill on the banks of the Sittang River. In spite of the casualties, Manekshaw captured Pagoda Hill, but in the process, he was severely injured in the machine gunfire. The doctors gave him a slim chance of survival; they had removed seven bullets from his body and most of his injured intestine. To everyone's surprise, Manekshaw recovered.

After the partition of India, Manekshaw was reassigned to the 8 Gorkha Rifles. When the Pakistani forces captured Muzaffarbad and Domel in Kashmir, Manekshaw, after a quick aerial survey, felt that only if the Indian troops were immediately deployed could they save Kashmir from being captured by the Pakistani army. His strong conviction resulted in Prime Minister Jawaharlal Nehru's permission. On 27 October 1947, the Indian troops moved into position and occupied Srinagar, even before the Pakistani forces could reach the outskirts of the city. The Pakistani forces were thwarted, and Manekshaw and the Indian Army became heroes.

The Indo-Pakistan War of 1971, a result of the Bangladesh Liberation War, saw Manekshaw at his best. East Pakistanis' demand of wanting complete autonomy from West Pakistan was turned down. The Pakistan Armed Forces launched a fierce attack on East Pakistan, resulting in a heavy death toll of the East Pakistanis. India joined forces with East Pakistan to help them form the new nation of Bangladesh.

With the courage of his convictions, Manekshaw told Prime Minister Indira Gandhi that they could win only if he was allowed to command his troops independently, without government interference. After receiving permission, Manekshaw devised his strategy. He started training a local militia group of Bengali nationalists, called the Mukti Bahini, training 75,000 guerrillas in warfare, equipping them with arms and ammunition. Three brigades of Bangladeshi troops were also trained.

When the war started on 3 December 1971, with the Pakistan aircraft bombing the Indian Air Force in the western part of the country, Manekshaw was ready with his strategy. Indian Army regiments entered from different directions: west, east, north and northeast, and with the assistance of the Indian Navy and Air Force, the Indian Army isolated the Pakistani forces and thwarted their attack by capturing all the major positions. In spite of Manekshaw making three radio addresses on three different days, 9, 11 and 15 December, asking the Pakistani troops to surrender, assuring them of an honourable treatment from his troops after their surrender, the war continued until Pakistan signed the Instrument of Surrender on 16 December 1971 and surrendered the eastern half, resulting in the formation of Bangladesh.

Manekshaw stuck to his words, showing kind-heartedness towards the 93,000 Pakistani soldiers who became prisoners of war. Manekshaw's appointment as the chief of the army staff from 8 June 1969 to 15 January 1973 shaped the Indian Army into a formidable war unit. He was the first Indian Army officer to be promoted to the rank of field marshal. Felicitated with many awards, including the Padma Bhushan, Padma Vibhushan and the Military Cross, in a career spanning more than 40 years, Sam Bahadur, as he was nicknamed, witnessed five wars.

Manekshaw died on 27 June 2008, leaving behind a legacy of bravery, paving the way for bravehearts to have the courage of their convictions and lead from the front.

41

SHAHNAZ HUSAIN

You Can Make Your Own Destiny

*D*estiny is a lot about free will. Many people can successfully lay claim to the fact that they made their own destiny. It's the choices one makes in life that determines the chances one gets. If one were to take a smooth path, with beautiful trees and flowers blooming on the sides, chances of encountering an exotic bird or seeing a rare flower blossom are higher than if one were to choose a rough path, filled with stones, with weeds and cactus blooming on the sides.

In the Mahabharata, both Karna and Abhimanyu made their destinies by choosing their own paths, though they were presented with the options. Several times, Karna (one of the best archers of his generation, whose archery skill was on par with the famed archer Arjuna's) was given the choice to leave Duryodhana, the eldest Kaurava prince, and join the Pandavas. But Karna stuck to Duryodhana's side in spite of knowing that his friend was wrong and was following the path of injustice. He also knew that Duryodhana was on the side of a losing team. The result was the complete annihilation of the Kauravas at the hands of the Pandavas; Karna's death became a war casualty.

Likewise for Abhimanyu, his knowledge of the chakravyuh (a deadly battle formation) was restricted to how to enter it or break into it, but he didn't know how to get out from it. He opted to enter the battle formation set up by Drona, and it proved fatal. He lost his life at the hands of the enemy. It is these choices that Karna and Abhimanyu made that determined their destinies.

Shahnaz Husain (nee Beg), the founder of The Shahnaz Husain Group, chose to make her own destiny and ended up giving India and the world the gift of a range of herbal cosmetics, popularizing the ancient culture of Ayurveda in the beauty industry.

She was born on 5 November 1944 in Samarkand, Uzbekistan, to Nasir Ullah Beg, the former chief justice of the Allahabad High Court, and Sayeeda Begum. Husain's maternal grandfather was the commander-in-chief of the Hyderabad army.

Husain had a pampered childhood. She studied in St. Mary's Convent in Allahabad. After she completed her matriculation, following the traditions of the family, at 15, Shahnaz was married to Nasir Husain, and a year later, she became a mother. With a caring husband and a loving child, life was perfect, but still there was a kind of restlessness in Husain. At the same time, she also had an urge to do something more in life. It was the 1960s, and Delhi was filled with women conducting a variety of courses. Husain tried her hand at many activities, from cooking to painting, even doing a course in interior decoration in an attempt to find her calling in life. The boredom continued until at a family friend's suggestion, she attended a beauty course. It not just interested her but changed her life. She had found her calling—the passion soon turned into an obsession to learn more.

Luckily for Husain, her husband, who was working with the State Trading Corporation, was sent to Tehran for a four-year posting. Tehran turned out to be the beauty Eden that Husain was seeking; it had all the major international beauty schools. Husain attended many beauty courses, contributing articles for the *Tehran Tribune*, to fund her learning. In London, while attending a course at the Helena Rubinstein Institute, Husain witnessed the damage caused by chemical-laden beauty products on a model.

The urge to change her destiny by achieving something was now joined by the urge to eliminate the damage chemicals wrecked on women's skin and hair. She constantly pondered over the need to find a safe alternative to beauty products. Around the same time, she had started studying Ayurveda, a subject that interested her. Her study of Ayurveda was a light-bulb moment; herbal beauty products were the perfect solution, providing the cure with the care of a mother's touch.

This was the catalyst that led her to launch her herbal salon and line of herbal products. With the firm belief that one can make one's own destiny, that one can be whatever one wanted to be, Husain started her first salon in the veranda of her home in New Delhi in 1977 by borrowing the starting capital of ₹35,000 from her father. The nameplate of this home-clinic was a small banner with Husain's name, qualifications and the services she provided, much like a local doctor's sign outside his clinic.

Even this small sign was sufficient to attract customers. Over the next few days, more and more clients poured in, as the word-of-mouth publicity spread. Customized beauty treatments appealed to many women. Things reached such a point that soon Husain removed the board. This also turned out to be the genesis of her no-advertisement policy—a good product is its own advertisement.

For centuries, Indian women only trusted the time-tested beauty products their mothers whipped up from their kitchen shelves for their skin and hair. Husain and her company turned out to be that mother with her cache of gentle products. This complete trust that people had in her cosmetics was a sign of her success.

Husain formulated products for specific skin and hair problems, like acne, pigmentation, dry skin, premature ageing, hair loss, dandruff, hair damage and dull hair, utilizing the goodness of plants, herbs, flowers, fruit extracts and essential oils to manufacture her cosmetics. Her state-of-the-art units with their focus on constant research and development gave her an edge over other brands.

Husain enabled many women to change their destinies by empowering them through her unique franchise system, where women received the training to provide treatments with her products in the comfort of their houses. These home-salons turned into small outlets selling her products, getting her brand more visibility.

It was the late 1980s. The beauty market in India was growing, and Husain capitalized on it by selling her products through a chain of distributors. From one herbal salon to a worldwide chain, the Shahnaz Husain Group's success story is truly remarkable. It wasn't unusual to see her cosmetics sitting cheek by jowl in department stores and beauty salons all over the world.

This Padma Shri awardee's dedication and hard work enabled her to translate her dreams into reality, with the belief that it's not what one wants in life but how badly one wants it that makes the difference. This motto helped her fulfil her desire of making her own destiny. Husain's life and career paved the way for the next generation of beauty entrepreneurs in India.

42

SHAKUNTALA DEVI

Discover Your Own Wonderland

Wonderlands, places full of beauty, have both a strange lure and a charm of their own. Alternatively called haven, paradise, dreamland, fairyland and enchanted world, it has attracted humankind into creating man-made wonderlands, which people can avail of at a price.

Though wonderland technically means an imaginary place of beauty and charm or a place that invokes awe and admiration, it's a magical place that can be a different place for different people. A wonderland could be a dreamworld where people disappear for hours on end. For scientists, a wonderland is their laboratory where they conduct path-breaking research and make discoveries. For artists, the dreamworld is their studio or the world of colours from where magical paintings emerge. For writers, it's the world of words and stories that transport readers into different places and time. For mathematicians, a dreamland is the world of numbers. The stage is a wonderland for actors.

One thing that is common in all these wonderlands is that it has the ability to transport the person to a different place by making them forget the real world. And in this make-believe place, great discoveries are made and geniuses emerge.

Shakuntala Devi, the mathematical genius, found her

wonderland in numbers, amazing the world with her calculating prowess, earning a place in *The Guinness Book of World Records*.

Shakuntala Devi was born on 4 November 1929 into a Kannada Brahmin family in Bangalore. Her father, C.V. Sundararaja Rao, worked in the circus, performing the roles of a trapeze artist, a tightrope walker, a magician and sometimes a lion tamer. The family faced many financial hardships; they couldn't afford to send their daughter to school, as the school fee of ₹2 was beyond their budget.

As her father also worked as a magician in the circus, he often amused his daughter with his magic tricks. One day, while showing the three-year-old Shakuntala Devi a card trick, he was surprised when she not just memorized the card sequence but also went a step ahead and calculated his next move. She did that repeatedly, surprising her father.

By the time Shakuntala Devi was five years old, her father, realizing that she was a child prodigy, left his circus job and started giving road shows where his young daughter displayed her prowess in calculation by solving complex mathematical problems in a few seconds. The young girl left the bystanders' mouths agape at her talent in multiplications. She could multiply with a speed that made the adults dizzy; while they were struggling to arrive at the right answers, Shakuntala Devi would already finish multiplying and give her answer. When the adults checked, they were stunned at the accuracy of her answer. It was as though the young girl had a calculator inside her head.

At the age of six, Shakuntala Devi displayed her jaw-dropping arithmetic abilities at the University of Mysore and several other universities, stunning the professors.

When Shakuntala Devi was 15, her family left India to settle in London. By now, Shakuntala Devi had started getting invitations to demonstrate her calculating skills at various institutes, returning after each session with a glow of happiness and pride, leaving the English flabbergasted at her numerical prowess. The world of numbers became Shakuntala Devi's private wonderland, where she would disappear for hours. It also gave her maximum happiness.

Over the next few years, Shakuntala Devi travelled all over the world, demonstrating her arithmetic talent. On 5 October 1950, in a BBC show hosted by Leslie Mitchell, he gave Shakuntala Devi a complicated mathematical problem, which she solved in a few seconds, stunning him. At first Mitchell believed that her answer was wrong, but when he rechecked, he realized that Shakuntala Devi's answer was correct and his own calculation was wrong. This news spread like wildfire, earning Shakuntala Devi the title of a Human Computer, a title she never warmed up to all her life. She believed that the human mind had more potential, more capabilities and was far superior to the computer.

Shakuntala Devi put the world in a quandary, leaving people constantly wondering how a woman who wasn't a mathematician or even educated could calculate such big numbers with ease. Sitting with a chalk in her hand, a board beside her, she demonstrated her affinity with numbers. Professors would shoot numbers at her, and before they even finished the question, she would have started writing the answer on the board, effortlessly calculating the cube root of 61,629,875, going several notches up and calculating the seventh root of 170,859,375. Her lightning-quick replies of 395 and 15 stunned the audience.

She demonstrated her skill before Albert Einstein in the early 1950s. Einstein asked Shakuntala Devi a question, which he took three hours to solve, as he had to follow the whole procedure with the step-by-step sequence to arrive at the right answer. If even a single step was missed, it would mess up the procedure. Einstein knew that nobody could solve that in less than three hours, as no one could jump from the question directly to the answer.

By the time Einstein had finished his question, Shakuntala Devi had started writing down the answer. The figures were so big that she took the whole board to write her answer. Einstein was puzzled because the lady sitting before him had just done the impossible. He asked her how she did it. Shakuntala Devi's reply that she didn't know how she did it, it simply happened, stunned Einstein. She further added that when Einstein asked her the question, figures started appearing before her eyes, somewhere inside she could see 1, 2, 3, and she just went on writing. It was as though her intuition was guiding her.

Shakuntala Devi returned to India sometime in the mid-1960s. By then, her fame had spread far and wide. She married an IAS officer, Paritosh Banerjee, and the couple had a daughter, Anupama.

In 1977, at the Southern Methodist University in Dallas, Shakuntala Devi was asked to calculate the 23rd root of a 20-digit number. While she did the calculation in 50 seconds, the US Bureau of Standards had to use the UNIVAC 1101 computer, writing a special programme into the computer to verify her answer—546,373,891. Needless to say, her answer was correct.

Over the years, she wrote several books on astrology, on the science of numbers and puzzles. Shakuntala Devi died on 21 April 2013 in Bangalore. A love of numbers that started at the age of three, continued all her life, immersing her in her private wonderland of numbers.

43

SUNDERLAL BAHUGUNA

Take the Macro Perspective

*I*t's only when the macro-perspective view aka the big-picture view is taken that one can see things in their entirety, unlike the micro perspective, which focuses on the individual. After floods and cyclones, when officials conduct an aerial survey of the area, it's because they want to take the macro perspective of the situation so as to get a clearer view of the entire city. The macro-perspective form of analysis makes one see the entire structure of society as a unified whole, enabling them to see the impact of a particular situation on society.

Vaccines are a result of the macro-perspective view, whereby the entire population is immunized against certain diseases. The concept of feminism, racism, sexism, Marxism and functionalism are all examples of the macro perspective, as they not just look at the working of a large section of society but also at how a certain event will affect that chunk of population. Macro perspective comprises long-term views, keeping long-term goals in mind.

One of the best examples of taking the macro perspective is the Quit India Movement led by Mahatma Gandhi, which, in turn, led to India's independence. Gandhi and all the freedom fighters kept the bigger picture in mind, every time their struggle met a roadblock. Once again, it was the same macro view that not only kept them going in the darkest of times but also motivated them throughout their struggle against the British Rule.

Sunderlal Bahuguna's macro-perspective view resulted in the Chipko movement in the 1970s. Bahuguna, a Garhwali environmentalist, fought for the preservation of the Himalayan forests for decades. Born on 9 January 1927 in Maroda village near Tehri in Uttarakhand, Bahuguna's social activism started when he was in his teens.

While growing up, Bahuguna saw his mother slogging every day—cooking, cleaning, washing and doing other household chores, with no respite. This affected him deeply, making him question the gender inequality between the sexes, sowing the seeds of activism in the young boy's mind, setting him on the path of fighting for women's rights and easing the burden from the shoulders of women in the villages.

When Bahuguna was 13 years old, he met the nationalist Shri Dev Burman, and under his tutelage, Bahuguna became an ardent supporter of Gandhi's philosophies and his path of non-violence, participating in India's independence struggle.

Before his marriage to Vimla Nautiyal in 1956, Bahuguna had a condition: they could only marry if she would live with him in the village after marriage and help him establish an ashram for the rural people. She agreed, and post their marriage, Bahuguna and his wife established the Silyara Ashram. One of their first missions was to educate the villagers about the importance of their natural resources and the threats these resources faced in the form of environmental degradation and destruction.

There was no shortage of causes for Bahuguna; he always took the macro view, seeing how certain things were affecting large sections of society. Seeing the plight of the hill women toiling hard to earn money, which their husbands squandered on liquor, bringing families on the brink of poverty, Bahuguna started the anti-liquor drive, gathering the hill women in his movement to eliminate the malaise of alcohol from the villages.

When the Government of India planned some developmental projects in the Himalayan regions and allocated the forest land to a company specializing in sports goods, Bahuguna trekked through the Himalayan forests, a journey of nearly 4,700 kilometres on foot, to assess the damage caused by these projects to the ecosystem of the Himalayas. He observed that such projects would affect the fauna and flora of the Himalayan regions; it would also have an impact on the life of the villagers living near these projects; deforestation would deprive the villagers of food and fuel, which the forest provided; it would also result in soil erosion, depletion of water resources, leading to an increased flooding in the area.

To prevent the cutting of trees, Bahuguna started the Chipko Andolan (movement) in April 1973 in Mandal village (now in Uttarakhand). The Chipko movement thrust Bahuguna into the activism limelight. Surprisingly, the idea for the Chipko movement was suggested by his wife.

When the government-backed logging started in the Himalayan forests, Bahuguna urged the villagers to embrace the trees to save them from being cut, as the trees belonged to the hills, had nurtured humanity like a mother, in innumerable ways, and should be saved at all cost. The word Chipko means 'to stick', and the villagers, especially women, joined forces with Bahuguna. When the forest contractors arrived with their tools to cut the trees, the local women started sticking to the trees, embracing them, some even tied themselves to the trees to prevent them from being chopped. This slowed down the government's work. Bahuguna coined the slogan of the Chipko movement: 'Ecology is permanent economy.'

The Chipko Andolan started garnering support from many villages, and resulted in hundreds of villagers joining Bahuguna.

This mass movement gathered so much force that it came under the media spotlight, leading to Bahuguna's meeting with Prime Minister Indira Gandhi, which resulted in the imposition of a 15-year ban on felling of green trees in the Himalayan forests in 1980.

Once again, Bahuguna took the macro perspective during the construction of the Tehri Dam, taking up a long crusade on behalf of the villagers. The Tehri Dam would destroy the ecosystem of the Himalayan regions; it would also displace thousands of villagers, endangering their lives, as it was located in a seismic zone. The purpose of the Tehri Dam was to divert the course of the Ganges River flowing down from the Himalayan mountains through the villages to increase its flow to the heavily populated city of New Delhi.

Bahuguna immediately saw the larger picture. This dam would affect the water supply in the mountain villages, affecting thousands of lives, causing them immense hardship. Following the principles of satyagraha, Bahuguna, the crusader of the Himalayan people, went on a hunger strike on the banks of the river Bhagirathi to mark his protest. Bahuguna's protest went on for over a decade; however, the project which was stalled due to the protest, resumed work in 2001. When the dam started to fill up in 2004, Bahuguna and his wife were shifted to their new home upstream by the government.

Bahuguna, a passionate eco-activist, was felicitated with many awards—the Padma Shri in 1981 (he refused to accept it), the Jamnalal Bajaj Award and the Padma Vibhushan. Bahuguna died on 21 May 2021 in Rishikesh. He spent his entire life being an eco-crusader, using the means of peaceful protest to make his point and bring major changes affecting a large section of society.

44

SUNIL CHHETRI

Make Discipline a Lifestyle

By studying Mother Nature, we realize her disciplined lifestyle. Wars, floods, tsunamis, earthquakes, cyclones, landslides, storms, riots, peace marches, protests, epidemics, pandemics—nothing in this universe prevents nature from following her routine. Nature's inbuilt alarm clock of sunrise and sunset continues to function with mechanical precision, on schedule—neither early nor late—every single day.

No calamity, no catastrophe, be it natural or man-made, can put nature on snooze mode; there are no pause buttons where nature's strict discipline is concerned. Nature's internal circadian rhythm of the four seasons—spring, summer, autumn and winter—seamlessly follow into one another, all over the world.

This discipline, both a marvel and a miracle, comes from the eternally optimistic attitude of nature. In spite of undergoing rampant cruelty from humanity, nature has clung on to its hopeful attitude. Every aspect of nature follows its cycle with precision. A seed becomes a tree. A larva turns into a caterpillar, which, in turn, transforms into a beautiful butterfly. A bud blossoms into a flower. The sun sets for the moon to rise.

The tiny green leaves and buds of spring blossom into the colourful flowers and the bright leaves of summer, the green leaves turn brown in autumn, giving way to the bleakness of winter. Once winter pushes spring forward, nature once again springs into action, erupting into tiny green shoots, and the cycle repeats itself.

There is a lot to learn from nature: be it her stoic behaviour or her resolute determination. Nature is one of the world's oldest tutors, teaching us every moment of the day. If we observe nature, absorb the lessons and discipline she is teaching us and emulate that optimistic trait, a disciplined lifestyle will follow us wherever we go.

Sunil Chhetri, professional football player and captain of the Indian national team, has not just adopted the discipline of nature but also made it his lifestyle. This strict discipline earned him the title of Captain Fantastic from the media and his fans. This disciplined approach has made Chhetri the highest goalscorer of the team, with a current tally of 80 goals in 126 matches and also the most-capped player.

Born on 3 August 1984 in Secunderabad, Telangana, Chhetri comes from a soccer-playing family—his father, Kharga Chettri, an officer in the Electronics and Mechanical Engineers Corps of the Indian Army, played in the army's football team. His mother, Sushila Chhetri, along with her twin sister, played in the women's national soccer team of Nepal. Football coursed through Chhetri's veins right from childhood. As a small boy, Chhetri would kick objects in his path, assuming them to be a ball. The result was many falls and bruises, but the young boy continued despite his injuries. He was especially attracted to footballs. Every time he saw a ball, getting restless, he would run towards it to kick it, dribble it across the ground, wherever he was, be it on the street, in a garden or a lawn or even inside a room. Initially, his parents dismissed this as just a craze, as all the boys in their family were crazy about football.

This passion grew with each passing day. After returning from school, Chhetri would hurriedly complete his homework before going out to play football with his friends. Dribbling past the big boys with ease, he would score goals after goals, making his team win. Even at that young age, Chhetri created nutmegs, effortlessly kicking the ball through his opponents' legs in his speedy journey towards the goalpost. Chhetri often played with his mother, and his attitude of always playing to win is inherited from her. She was a fierce rival, not ceding an inch, even though she was playing with her son.

Chhetri lived in several places due to his father's frequent transfers: Secunderabad, Gangtok, Darjeeling, Calcutta and New Delhi; his schooling too happened in different places, Bahai School in Gangtok, Army Public School in Delhi and Ashutosh College in Calcutta.

Chhetri's professional career started in 2002 with Mohun Bagan. After completing his schooling, Chhetri said goodbye to studies to take up professional football. Two years later, Chhetri was a part of the Indian U-20 team. His two goals against Bhutan resulted in India's 4-1 silver medal victory in the 2004 South Asian Federation Games.

Chhetri's international debut happened on 12 June 2005, when he played for the national team against Pakistan. The coach, Sukhwinder Singh, was in a dilemma. His best player, Bhaichung Bhutia, was missing due to an injury. Singh reluctantly allowed an injured Chhetri to play in the team. The match started in Ayub Stadium in Quetta, and in the 65th minute, Chhetri collected the ball from inside the penalty area and kicked it past the goalkeeper, scoring his first goal and earning a place in the team.

This was the start of his goalscoring hunger, getting him the title of AIFF (All India Football Federation) Player of the Year six times—in 2007, 2011, 2013, 2014, 2017 and 2018–19. The 2007 Nehru Cup was one of his best performances, making

Chhetri the top scorer for India; his four goals helped India win the cup.

Always in a learning mode, Chhetri never lets a day pass without training. Once on a holiday to Ooty, on the first day itself, Chhetri was doing push-ups on the floor of his hotel room. Chhetri redefines discipline. He measures his food, literally down to a grain, to his body's requirement. Culinary indulgences are taboo for Chhetri, for he believes that the sacred temple of the body must be kept in good condition at all times.

Whether he is playing football, ludo or monopoly; whether he is playing with an international team or a casual game with family or friends, Chhetri hates to lose. This attitude is the reason for his stellar performance in the Indian Super League—as winger and striker, he has claimed many victories for his teams.

Chhetri became the first Indian to play in the Major League Soccer when he played for the Kansas City Wizards. As of 28 May 2022, Chhetri is the second-highest international goalscorer along with Lionel Messi.

Chhetri's obsession with the game is so high that every time he is injured, he becomes grumpy until he recovers and is back on the field to score more goals and dribble his nutmegs. A big self-motivator, he believes in mental fitness, and to strengthen it, he watches motivational videos and reads books.

Winner of the Arjuna Award, Major Dhyan Chand Khel Ratna Award and the Padma Shri, Chhetri's personal philosophy that every time one falls, one must rise again, is the reason for his enthusiastic attitude, to his game, to life. The boy who kicked any ball he could find has become a role model for football lovers, dribbling his way into their hearts.

45

TARLA DALAL

Keep It Simple

*H*aven't we seen how in fairy tales the simple girl-next-door rides away into the sunset with the handsome prince, leaving her extravagantly dolled-up sisters watching the scene in shock and their jaws nearly touching the floor? What was it about the plain girl that her sisters couldn't replicate? It was simplicity which won over the prince. Simplicity has a beauty of its own.

It's the simple pleasures of life that give one immense joy—watching the sunset, staring at the clouds, licking one's fingers after eating a hearty meal, screaming uninhibitedly on a merry-go-round, slurping the milky tea from the roadside dhaba or slugging the creamy lassi leaving its milky trail in the form of a white moustache and later licking the milk moustache. Simplicity has a joy of its own, and the ensuing happiness is its biggest reward.

The simple formula finds its biggest advocate in KISS, which was originally an acronym for 'keep it simple, stupid', later other derivates entered popular usage, like 'keep it stupid simple', 'keep it short and simple', 'keep it simple and straightforward', and 'keep it simple, silly'. But we will change the word stupid to smartie. Because smart people make simple things work for them.

The concept of KISS was coined by an aircraft engineer

who worked in a company that manufactured Lockheed U-2 and SR-71 Blackbird spy planes. While handing his team of designers a set of tools, the aircraft designer challenged his team with the KISS principle, instructing them that the fighter planes they were designing must be easy to repair by an average mechanic under stressful and time-constraining conditions of the battlefield. Software developers utilize this principle a lot.

Closer home, chef Tarla Dalal adopted this principle in a big way in her cooking. One could also say that it was the hallmark of her recipes. Dalal was born on 3 June 1936 in Pune into a Gujarati family. She had a normal childhood, spending her time studying and helping her mother with the kitchen chores. By the age of 12, Dalal had become the home chef's assistant. After her matriculation, Dalal did a BA in economics.

Tarla's culinary talent came to the forefront after her marriage to Nalin Dalal. It was while her husband was doing his master's in chemical engineering in America that Dalal got the opportunity to switch her roles, from being her mother's helper to handling the kitchen all by herself. In a new country, with nothing much to do, she rustled up three to four new recipes every day, cooking them again and again until she had earned her husband's approval and was satisfied with the outcome.

After her return to India, Dalal followed her personal philosophy of sharing good things with everyone by starting cooking classes at her South Bombay residence. The initial handful of students soon swelled to a big crowd. Her cooking classes gained so much traction that at one time, it became mandatory for unmarried girls to learn their cooking skills from Dalal before stepping into their marital households. Her classes assured the parents of their daughters' proficiency and excellence in the culinary art that would come in handy in their new house.

Dalal's recipes were simple both in the procedure followed

to make a dish and in the ingredients used. It was this twin advantage that made her a firm favourite. Thousands of newly wedded young girls entered their marital homes armed with a handful of Dalal's cookbooks as their kitchen friends, referring to the books, both for their day-to-day cooking as well as for whipping up delectable dishes for their guests.

It's said that the way to a man's heart is through his stomach. Actually, we can tweak that saying: the way to anyone's heart is through their stomachs. Dalal's recipes gained nationwide following. North Indians whipped up sambar and idlis with a variety of chutneys, upma and pongal, while south Indian homemakers amazed their families with paneer butter masala, chole bhature, melt-in-the-mouth malai koftas and mutter paneer. Pan-India, women learnt to make gulab jamuns, malpuas and barfis by following her recipes.

Dalal's motto of keeping it simple and straightforward followed her throughout her career and in all the cuisines in which she experimented. Women the world over didn't have to scramble around for expensive ingredients to rustle up delicacies. The handful of items lying in their kitchen shelves was sufficient to produce droolworthy dishes.

Though Dalal's forte was Gujarati cuisine, she experimented with a variety of cuisines, constantly innovating to keep up with people's changing tastes. She introduced western cuisine to Indians by modifying these dishes with locally available ingredients. She converted non-vegetarian dishes into delicious vegetarian ones by replacing the meat with paneer, potato, corn and mushroom.

To make her recipes available to a wider audience who couldn't attend her cooking classes, Dalal published her first cookbook, *The Pleasures of Vegetarian Cooking*, in 1974. It was such a huge hit that she went on to write 170 cookbooks, selling more than 10 million copies, making her one of the top five bestselling cookery authors in the world. Dalal's books were translated into many Indian as well as foreign languages. At one time, every household had several of Dalal cookbooks, and the often-used books were a testimony to the success of her recipes, which had the gentle touch of a mother's and a grandmother's cooking.

With global fans came the need for conducting cookery classes around the world, and Dalal, armed with her cache of recipes, travelled around the world, training eager students. In the latter part of her life, she focused on healthy cooking, whipping up zero-oil and low-calorie variants of popular dishes and sweets to cater to her health-conscious fans battling a variety of health issues, from diabetes to cholesterol and heart ailments.

A constant innovator, she started a bimonthly magazine, *Cooking & More*. Filled with her trademark simple recipes that could be whipped up by novices, it delighted her ever-widening fans. And when she started her cookery show, thousands of viewers tuned in to *Cook It Up With Tarla Dalal*. The kitchen queen was on a roll.

She was the only cookbook author to be felicitated with the Padma Shri by the Indian government. Dalal died of a heart attack on 6 November 2013 in Mumbai, leaving the legacy of her simple but delicious recipes as her memories in the culinary world.

46

VERGHESE KURIEN

Invoke the Perseverance Trait

To keep at something despite the delays in achieving success is a sign of perseverance. Though it's a quality easily available, not many avail its benefits. This quality defines achievers. Behind every winner lies the sturdy wall of perseverance, constantly providing support in difficult times.

Sati Savitri's name has become synonymous with persistence. King Asvapati ruling over Madra Kingdom and his wife, Queen Malavi, were childless. They prayed to the Sun God named Savitr. The Sun God blessed them with a baby girl. King Asvapati and his queen named their daughter Savitri in honour of the God whose blessings had led to her birth.

When the beautiful Savitri reached marriageable age, her personality and beauty intimidated prospective suitors, making them reluctant to ask for her hand in marriage. Her concerned father suggested that Savitri go on a mission to find a husband for herself. In the course of her search, Savitri met an exiled King Dyumatsena, blinded and thrown out from his kingdom of Salwa, living in the forest with his wife and son Satyavan. Savitri chose Satyavan as her husband. According to a prophecy, Satyavan was supposed to die exactly a year later. After marrying Satyavan, Savitri moved to the forest to live with him. Exactly on the prophesized date, Satyavan fell unconscious.

When Yama, the lord of death, came to claim Satyavan's soul, Savitri followed him as he walked to the other world, pleading and reasoning with him. Yama constantly urged her to go back, but Savitri, undaunted by the powerful god of death, trailed him. Impressed with her perseverance, Yama offered her a boon. Savitri immediately asked for a hundred sons for Satyavan and herself, putting Yama in a dilemma. He had no option but to bring Satyavan back to life so that his boon could be fulfilled.

If Verghese Kurien hadn't displayed his trait of perseverance, there would have been no Amul, a name synonymous with an array of milk products in India.

Kurien was born on 26 November 1921 in Calicut (now Kozhikode), Kerala, into a Syrian Christian family. A good student, after completing his schooling, Kurien joined Loyola College in Madras for his BSc. His father, a civil surgeon in a government hospital, inspired his choice of subjects—science, especially physics. At every stage of his education, Kurien was the youngest in his class. This instilled in him both a fiercely independent streak and the confidence to handle any situation—two traits that would come in handy in his career.

After getting his bachelor's degree in mechanical engineering from the College of Engineering, Guindy, Kurien was keen on joining the army as an engineer, but he ended up joining the Tata Steel Technical Institute, Jamshedpur, at his mother's insistence. With an urge to do more in life, Kurien applied for a government scholarship for his master's. Luckily, he got the scholarship, but in dairy engineering. When Kurien reached the Michigan State University in America to do his master's degree, he chose a few dairy electives so that he wouldn't be breaking his scholarship rules but opted for mechanical engineering (metallurgy).

After completing his master's, Kurien returned to India, and as a part of his bond agreement, was sent by the Indian government to its old creamery in Anand, a town in Kaira district of Gujarat. Initially disinterested, Kurien nevertheless stayed put, using his mechanical engineering degree to advantage by studying all the old machines, often repairing them when they broke down.

But destiny had other plans. When he was on the verge of quitting his job, he met the freedom fighter and social reformer Tribhuvandas Kishibhai Patel. Patel requested Kurien to help him with the cooperative society he had started to prevent the exploitation of the dairy farmers by the milk distributors. The farmers' plight and struggle tugged at Kurien's heartstrings. Leaving his government job, Kurien joined Patel in the Kaira District Co-operative Milk Producers' Union Ltd (KDCMPUL), which was later renamed Amul Dairy.

The Amul cooperative directly linked dairy farmers in villages to the consumers in Bombay, eliminating the need for middlemen and the big commissions they charged. It wasn't unusual to see a long line of farmers transporting their milk via village roads, called milk roads or a cold-chain, to consumers in Bombay. This became a win-win situation for both the farmers and the consumers—the farmers had a regular income and the consumers, good-quality milk at a decent price.

This was the start of the White Revolution in India, called Operation Flood or the Billion-litre idea. It became the world's largest agriculture dairy development programme. It was due to Kurien's tenacity and perseverance that India turned from a milk-deficient country to the largest producer of milk in the world. The Anand pattern of dairy cooperatives became a role model, getting replicated all over India under the umbrella of the National Dairy Development Board (NDDB).

Kurien now faced a new problem. In some seasons, the farmers ended up with a surplus milk production. This extra milk got spoilt if not immediately delivered to the customers. Kurien came up with the idea of turning this surplus milk into milk powder that could be stored. Now Kurien had another problem in his hand. The surplus milk was buffalo milk, which was thicker than cow's milk, and dairy experts considered it unsuitable for producing milk powder. But Kurien managed to do the unthinkable. Taking the help of his batchmate from America, H.M. Dalaya, he not just made milk powder but also condensed milk. Later, Kurien utilized the same buffalo milk to produce cheese, further branching into butter. To bring down the overall costs, he set up a packaging unit at the cooperative.

Throughout his long career, Kurien, considering himself an employee of the dairy farmers, worked hard for them, always thinking for their betterment, keeping their interests above anything else. At times, the struggle became real, as Kurien had to battle political interferences, bureaucracy and the monopoly of bigger companies. Kurien was unrelenting in his vision of making milk a tool for the economic development of India, for making dairy farming India's largest self-sustaining industry and for improving the financial conditions of the farmers by increasing their incomes and ridding them of their debts.

Felicitated with many awards, such as the Padma Shri, Padma Bhushan, Padma Vibhushan, Ordre du Mérite Agricole (Order of Agricultural Merit) from the French government, World Food Prize, Krishi Ratna Award and Ramon Magsaysay Award, Kurien's birthday on 26 November is celebrated as National Milk Day.

Kurien died on 9 September 2012 in Anand. His perseverance, despite the odds stacked against him, saw Amul become India's largest food brand and deservingly bag the title of The Taste of India and Kurien, the title of The Milkman of India.

47

VIKRAM SARABHAI

Take the Road Less Travelled

> *Two roads diverged in a wood, and I—*
> *I took the one less travelled by,*
> *And that has made all the difference.*

This stanza from the poem 'The Road Not Taken' by Robert Frost has come to define people who set out on previously unchartered terrain. Over the years, these lines have become synonymous with people who have thought independently, broken away from the tight confines of convention and the traditional way of doing things, made daring choices, stuck to their guns despite the naysayers and mounting obstacles, and started out on a new road—a road less travelled.

More often than not, we take the well-trodden path in life for reasons of safety, for the assurance of seeing familiar sights; these paths smoothened by years of different peoples' footsteps and illuminated by the knowledge of the early explorers' experiences are also filled with fellow travellers with whom we can exchange stories.

There are all kinds of fears when we chart unknown territories, traverse new roads, move over strange waters that may be either too shallow or too deep and infested with sharks, but unless and until we take the risk, newer destinations just cannot be reached. But once traversed, the footprints we leave behind on the path inspire and motivate generations of fellow travellers to take the same path. The footprints also serve as a constant reminder that if it can be done once, it can be done again; all it needs is the courage to take that first step into the unknown. There are always a few brave souls who, by travelling on an unknown path, end up making a track for the next generation to follow.

Vikram Sarabhai, a visionary, a man far ahead of his times, took many roads less travelled, giving India several firsts. Regarded as the Father of the Indian Space Programme, Sarabhai, a physicist and an astronomer, was instrumental in establishing the space research programme in India and also in developing nuclear power in India.

Sarabhai was born on 12 August 1919 in Ahmedabad into the affluent Sarabhai family, which owned mills and industries, and was an active participant in India's independence struggle. After graduating from Gujarat College in Ahmedabad, Sarabhai studied at the University of Cambridge in England, taking his tripos in natural sciences in 1940. Cambridge beckoned once again and Sarabhai returned there in 1945 to complete his doctorate; the subject of his thesis was 'Cosmic Ray Investigations in Tropical Latitudes'.

On returning to India in 1947, Sarabhai founded the Physical Research Laboratory (PRL), an institute for scientific research at his residence, as a charitable trust, with his family and friends contributing the funds. PRL, considered the womb of space sciences in India, focused on the study of cosmic rays.

Several months later, Sarabhai moved PRL to the M.G. Science Institute, Ahmedabad, and later, with grants from the Atomic Energy Commission of India, he broadened the focus of PRL's research to studying the properties of the upper atmosphere, theoretical physics and radio physics.

After reading about the Russians launching their satellite Sputnik, Sarabhai appealed to the Indian government, saying that to tap India's potential to be on the moon, it needed an institute specializing in space programmes. With the Nehru government's approval, Sarabhai set up the Indian National Committee for Space Research (INCOSPAR) in 1962. It was later renamed the Indian Space Research Organisation (ISRO).

Sarabhai was just 28 years old when he and physicist Homi Bhabha set up India's first rocket launching station, starting the project and thereby leading to the construction of India's first satellite Aryabhata. It was launched on 19 April 1975 from Kapustin Yar, a Russian rocket launch site (cosmodrome), a few years after Sarabhai's death.

Along with Homi Bhabha, Sarabhai set up India's first rocket launching station—the Thumba Equatorial Rocket Launching Station (TERLS) in Thumba, Thiruvananthapuram. It launched its first rocket, the Nike-Apache made by NASA, on 21 November 1963. Parts of this rocket were ferried to the launch pad in a bullock cart and on the back of a bicycle. TERLS was later renamed Vikram Sarabhai Space Centre. It has a quaint history. Sarabhai had selected a small fishing village named Thumba as the location for a rocket launching station, and the spot he had chosen was the site of a church—the St Mary Magdalene Church. Sarabhai and his team met the bishop of Trivandrum. When the team showed an interest in acquiring the church land, the bishop asked them to attend the Sunday mass. At the mass attended by the scientists, the bishop announced Sarabhai's request of needing God's abode as a place for his rocket launch. The bishop explained that both the scientists and spiritual preachers were seeking the truth, but from different angles and places. The congregation agreed with the bishop, and Sarabhai got his launch pad. After ensuring that the villagers were shifted to a new village and received a new church, the rocket launching station was built.

On one side, Sarabhai steered the family business to greater success, on the other hand, he established organizations that were the need of the hour—Operations Research Group (ORG), the first market research organization in India; Darpana Academy for Performing Arts with his wife Mrinalini, a classical dancer; and ATIRA (Ahmedabad Textile Industry's Research Association).

With an eye on the future, realizing that management institutes would play a key role in the educational development of the country, Sarabhai established the Indian Institute of Management (IIM) in Ahmedabad in 1962.

After Homi Bhabha's death in 1966, Sarabhai, appointed chairman of the Atomic Energy Commission of India, carried forward Bhabha's work in nuclear research, establishing several nuclear power plants, which played a huge role in developing nuclear technology for defence purposes. Passionate about space programmes, Sarabhai established many institutes: the Vikram Sarabhai Space Centre in Thiruvananthapuram, the Space Applications Centre in Ahmedabad, in which six institutions established by him were merged, the Fast Breeder Test Reactor (FBTR) in Kalpakkam, the Variable Energy Cyclotron Centre (VECC) in Calcutta, the Electronics Corporation of India Limited (ECIL) in Hyderabad and Uranium Corporation of India Limited (UCIL) in Jaduguda, Jharkhand.

Felicitated with the Padma Bhushan and, in 1972, posthumously with the Padma Vibhushan, Sarabhai's brilliant career was cut short when he died of a heart attack on 30 December 1971 in his hotel room in Kovalam, Kerala, while visiting Thiruvananthapuram to lay the foundation stone of the

Thumba railway station. Earlier in the day, he had watched the launch of a Russian rocket.

Sarabhai, a man far ahead of his times, constantly anticipating the future needs of the country, travelled on unchartered roads to start several institutions, laying the foundation of future scientific advancements in India.

48

VINOBA BHAVE

Stand up for What You Believe In

'Stand up for what you believe in, even if you are standing alone.' This quote by Sophie Scholl motivates one to stand up or be vocal for what they believe is the right thing in life.

King Ashoka (r. 265 to 238 BCE), called Ashoka the Great, was a firm believer in standing up for what he believed in. Belonging to the Maurya dynasty, grandson of Chandragupta Maurya, founder of the Maurya dynasty, Ashoka expanded his kingdom through a series of aggressive conquests. At one time, his kingdom covered practically the entire Indian subcontinent, with the exception of a few places, stretching from present-day Bangladesh in the east to Afghanistan in the north-west. With its capital at Pataliputra, Ashoka's empire was a force to reckon with.

The turning point in Ashoka's life came when he waged the Kalinga War to conquer more territories. The mass-scale deaths turned the waters of the Daya River red with blood and the destruction he saw, resulted in a change of heart, with Ashoka renouncing war as a means of conquest. So strong was the transformation in him that he converted to Buddhism, adopting the policy of *dhamma* (meaning, dharma in Sanskrit). Dhamma was a set of rules for the subjects of his kingdom: people should live in peace and harmony, love others, should practise the path of ahimsa (non-violence) and should show respect and tolerance for all religions. Ashoka travelled throughout his empire to spread this message to his subjects, even appointing dharma ministers. From a war-waging king, he transformed into a king with a social conscience, building hospitals for humans and animals, planting trees, digging wells, and constructing rest houses and watersheds. To propagate Buddhism, he built stupas, pillars and monasteries.

Vinayak Narahari Bhave or Vinoba Bhave is a perfect example of 'stand up for what you believe in'. In fact, he went a whole lot further than just standing up for what he believed in; he walked for his beliefs, bringing to the collective notice of the entire nation, the social injustices prevalent in society. An advocate of non-violence, Bhave was a human rights activist and a social activist, even before the words became popular.

Bhave was born on 11 September 1895 in Gagoji village in Kolaba, Maharashtra. Bhave and his five siblings—four brothers and a sister—were introduced to the Bhagavad Gita by their deeply religious mother, Rukmini Devi, at a young age. As he grew older, Bhave studied it in more detail under his grandfather. Soon, the Bhagavad Gita became Bhave's guiding philosophy, his spiritual conscience; he considered it his life's breath. His father, Narahari Shambhu Rao's rational thinking too shaped his outlook.

Though Bhave was a good student in school, with mathematics being his main interest, he had little fondness for traditional education with their strict adherence to textbook learning. At one time, he even wanted to move to the Himalayas as a renunciate.

Bhave treated the world as his oyster, travelling all over India, learning local languages, acquiring knowledge of the scriptures. While he was in Benares, he read Mahatma Gandhi's speech in the newspaper. Something changed for Bhave. This was the moment he was subconsciously waiting for.

Bhave burnt his school and college certificates, and wrote a letter to Gandhi. This exchange of letters continued until, at Gandhi's suggestion, the young Bhave met Gandhi at the Kochrab Ashram in Ahmedabad on 7 June 1916. He joined the ashram, absorbing Gandhi's teaching, learning by osmosis, and he started living a life of austerity.

Gandhi became one of the biggest influences in Bhave's life, almost a father figure. Following Gandhi's footsteps, Bhave became a crusader for India's independence from evils like untouchability and inequality. Seeing Bhave's keenness, Gandhi entrusted him with greater responsibilities, sending him to take charge of the Wardha ashram and entrusting him with the supervision of Harijans at a temple in Vaikom, Kerala.

Even though Bhave participated in the civil disobedience movement against the British and was even jailed with many nationalists, he was little known to the outside world. It was only after Gandhi chose Bhave as the first satyagrahi (an individual standing up for truth) against the British rule on 5 October 1940 that Bhave rose to prominence.

Bhave's religious outlook was broad, his thinking progressive. Jai Jagat (meaning, victory to the world)—the slogan he coined not just summed up his world views but also became his motto in life. Bhave saw the world as a whole, and the people without distinction. Going a step further, Bhave adopted Gandhi's term Sarvodaya (meaning, progress of all), making it the genesis of his myriad social-reform programmes. Bhave endorsed social equality. It pained him to see India's agricultural economy in the grip of a few rich landowners, with the poor farmers toiling hard for paltry earnings, while the landlords pocketed the profits.

To balance this inequality, Bhave started the Bhoodan movement (Land Gift movement) on 18 April 1951 in Pochampally village (present-day Telangana). After Bhave met

80 Harijan families who requested 80 acres of land to make a living, Bhave mulled over how he could get the land for them. He then came up with the idea of asking the wealthy landowners to give a small percentage of their land to landless people. At Bhave's request, a landlord offered the required land. This was the beginning of the movement.

Bhave travelled all over India for 13 years, covering 58,741 kilometres, asking people with land to consider him as one of their sons and give him one-sixth of their land. He would appeal to the people, 'I have come to loot you with love. If you have four sons, consider me your fifth and give me my share.'

The donated land would be distributed to landless farmers. The beneficiary farmers were bound by the Bhoodan Act, stipulating that they had no right to sell the land but to only use it for agricultural purpose. The Bhoodan movement gained global attention; it was a unique example of social justice achieved through a peaceful march. Post the Bhoodan movement, Bhave started the Gramdam movement (village in gift), asking for whole villages as donations, accumulating more than 1,000 villages.

Bhave believed that by serving people he was worshipping God, as everything was but a manifestation of God. He spent the latter part of his life at the Brahma Vidya Mandir, an ashram he started in Paunar in Wardha (Maharashtra). He died on 15 November 1982 at his ashram in Wardha.

Bhave was the first recipient of the Ramon Magsaysay Award for Community Leadership, and he received the Bharat Ratna posthumously in 1983.

Popularly called Acharya ('teacher' in Sanskrit), Bhave adopted peaceful means to bring a social revolution.

49

Y.K. HAMIED

Sometimes Put Others before Yourself

Mothers the world over are synonymous with putting others' welfare before their own. And this trait of motherhood cuts across species. Bird mothers fly for miles to look for food for their chicks. A lioness is fiercely protective of her cubs. As is a mother bear.

An elephant mother is one of the most protective animal mothers on this planet. Herds of female elephants and their children usually travel in a circle, with the youngest ones kept safe inside the circle, to protect them from predators. Emperor penguin mothers travel for nearly 50 miles to the ocean front to catch fishes for their chick, later regurgitating the caught fish to the hatched chick, who is left in the safe custody of the male.

And when the focus is on a human mother, she beats the other species hollow when it comes to putting others before herself. The protection of her offspring brings out the fierce aspect of her personality to the forefront.

One trait differentiating heroes from common people is the ability to put others before themselves. This attribute is intrinsic to heroes. Without batting an eyelid, these heroes in uniforms transform themselves into human shields. You guessed it right. The heroes we are discussing here are our armed forces. These heroes minus the capes not only take the enemies' bullets but also lay down their lives to save their motherland as well as protect their brethren from enemy attacks. Doctors, firemen, policemen, all show the traits of heroes, putting their lives at risk every day.

Yusuf Khwaja Hamied or Y.K. Hamied did just that—put the welfare of others above his company's profit. And this altruistic trait of his made him a hero. Hamied, a Polish-born Indian scientist was the chairman of Cipla Limited, an Indian generics pharmaceuticals company set up by his father Khwaja Abdul Hamied in 1935.

Hamied was born on 25 July 1936, in Vilnius, Lithuania, to an Indian Muslim father and a Lithuanian Jew mother. Brought up in India, after completing his schooling and college in Bombay, Hamied left for England to do his PhD in organic chemistry from Christ's College in Cambridge. Returning to India, he joined his father's company as a research and development officer. His father ensured that Hamied earned his stripes; he was paid his first salary only after he had completed one year at Cipla.

Taking over the company after his father's death, Hamied started working towards his goal of making medicines affordable for all. He introduced around 30 bulk drugs and their formulations, becoming a pioneer of the bulk drug industry in India, making Cipla a leader in the domestic pharmaceutical industry. Cipla not just manufactured an array of medicines for the local market, it also exported its medicines to more than 180 countries.

Under Hamied, Cipla became the first Indian pharmaceutical company to make API (active pharmaceutical ingredient)—the active chemical components in medicines—enabling his company to become self-sufficient in drug manufacturing.

When the lethal HIV virus hit Africa, Hamied made the world's health community sit up by declaring that his company could produce the generic drugs for AIDS treatment at the cost of

$1 per day, which was at that time a very small fraction of what the pharmaceutical companies in the West were charging for the same medicines. Not only did Hamied single-handedly break the stranglehold of big drug companies, he also showed the world that AIDS drugs didn't require a fat wallet. His announcement forced the big drug companies to drop the price of their medicines to be able to compete with Hamied.

Hamied's largesse of supplying this triple combination ARV (antiretroviral) treatment resulted in saving thousands of patients' lives in the underdeveloped countries. Hamied ensured that besides the AIDS drugs, patients in poor countries also received life-saving medicines for other ailments at a price much less than what other pharmaceutical companies were charging. Along the way, Hamied also changed the world's perception that Indian generic drugs were poor-quality knock-offs of the original drugs.

Hamied set up CiplaQCIL in Uganda; approved by the World Health Organization, this factory was a collaboration between Cipla and the Ugandan government, and produced ARV as well as antimalarial drugs, resulting in Uganda's self-sufficiency where healthcare was concerned. Hamied also announced that he was ready to give the formula to make this ARV free of cost to any company willing to produce its own drugs. Hamied also offered to provide nevirapine, the drug limiting HIV transmission from mother to child, for free—an unheard of gesture from a drug manufacturing company.

This billionaire businessman has often said that he doesn't want to make money from diseases that damage the entire fabric of society. His reasoning being that if he doesn't make money on a few drugs, it's not a cause for concern because it's more important to keep people alive and nations stable, as illnesses, especially epidemics, cause havoc to economies, destabilizing nations.

Hamied holds his chemistry notebooks from Cambridge close

to his heart, often referring to them while developing new syntheses of drugs. He is credited with pioneering the development of the multidrug combination pills, known in the medical world as FDCs or fixed-dose combination pills, especially for HIV/AIDS, tuberculosis (TB), asthma and several paediatric drugs, which have become a blessing for children in poorer countries. These innovations made by Hamied have resulted in greater drug safety by ensuring that these medicines are taken in their proper dosages.

With several research papers and international patents to his name, Hamied's mission in life is to create low-cost biotech drugs for the treatment of cancer, diabetes and many other chronic diseases, thereby reducing the price of medicines, making it accessible to the needy. He endorses the view that for critical drugs, multinational companies should voluntarily enter into a licencing agreement with local companies, allowing them to manufacture these drugs on a royalty payment. This will bring down the cost of the medicines.

Hamied, a Padma Bhushan awardee, did the unthinkable by swimming against the tide of manufacturing medicines for profits by putting the lives of others above his company's profit, and selling medicines without worrying about financial gains. He showed the world that a pharma company could be a life saviour in more ways than one can imagine. Hamied's gesture is worthy of genuflection and his name makes every Indian's heart swell with pride.

50

ZUBIN MEHTA

Keep Your Sense of Awe and Wonder Alive

A sense of awe and wonder is what separates tourists from regular people. They display this emotion while soaking in the sights and sounds of a new culture, as though they are memorizing it for posterity. So often we overlook the buildings in our city, passing frequently near them, but unable to notice the beauty of their visual grandeur. But tourists take their time to admire each and every aspect of the same monument that local citizens overlook.

The reason for this sense of awe and wonder is that the tourists leave the gates of their senses wide open, allowing the sights and sounds around them to stir all their senses. These tourists are like sponges, with a keenness to learn and absorb what they are seeing and experiencing. Unlike the citizens who have closed their senses to these visual, olfactory and auditory delights of their cities, courtesy of the rat race and the monotonous daily routine, tourists, visiting with a purpose, let whatever they see transport them to a state of enchantment, making them float on a carpet of an unexplainable emotion.

Zubin Mehta, conductor of western and eastern classical

music, never let go of his sense of awe and wonder in his music. It was this trait that made him one of the greatest orchestra conductors in the world. His technical mastery over music was complemented by the delight he took in it every single day, every time he appeared on stage.

Mehta was born on 29 April 1936 in Bombay into a Parsi family. In childhood, Mehta was exposed to his father Mehli's music. His father, a violinist and founder of the Bombay Symphony Orchestra, had a habit of daily practice. Mehta grew up with music floating around him, inspiring him to emulate his father. Small children are usually fascinated with toys; Mehta was enchanted with music and musical instruments. Seeing his son's inclination and passion, his father taught him to play the piano and the violin.

Mehta started training as a conductor in his teens. He often led a few rehearsals of certain sections of the Bombay Symphony conducted by his father. Under the watchful eyes of his brilliant father, Mehta honed his skills as a conductor. By the time he was 16, his father had groomed him so well that Mehta started conducting the full orchestra during rehearsals. Mehta's sense of awe and wonder, which had by now become a sixth sense, sharpened his skills.

Post his schooling from St. Mary's School, Bombay, Mehta enrolled to study medicine at St. Xavier's College at his mother's insistence; she considered medicine a better choice of career than music. Luckily, Mehta didn't think like her. Two years of medicine were enough for the 18-year-old Mehta to drop out of college and leave for Vienna, Europe's prestigious music centre.

At the Vienna Academy of Music, Mehta studied under Hans Swarowsky, mastering the double bass and soaking everything like a sponge. Alongside his studies, Mehta participated in international competitions, winning most of them. When he won the first prize in the Liverpool International Conductor's Competition by defeating 100 contestants, as a part of his prize, he conducted the Royal Liverpool Philharmonic as an associate conductor. He was just 21.

That was the start of Mehta's journey. The concerts he conducted won him rave reviews, leaving the music world stunned at the young man's talent. Within a few years, Mehta started substituting for music maestros of the world, gaining valuable experience, honing his skills as a conductor and also winning the hard-to-please critics. Each and every prestigious symphony he conducted brought on a new wave of awe and wonder at music, its effect on his senses and on the audience.

When Mehta became the music director of the Los Angeles Philharmonic at 26, he had a clear vision of what he wanted to do. The Los Angeles Philharmonic Orchestra was a big orchestra of talented musicians. Mehta's aim was to bring out the best from the individual musicians and also the whole orchestra. Mehta, with his intuitive music knowledge, first shifted the musicians from their earlier places. Then he juggled their assignments like a music magician. These changes imbued the orchestra's music with serene warmth and a much-needed richness, leaving the audience perpetually enthralled.

The music emerging from cellos, violins and basses put Mehta in a constant state of wonder, letting their tunes transport him into a different world from where he created mesmerizing music with the wave of his wand. He was only in his twenties when he conducted the Vienna Philharmonic and the Berlin Philharmonic, considered two of the greatest orchestras in the world. For a concert in Vienna, Mehta earned a 20-minute-long standing ovation, 14 curtain calls and two encores.

Mehta's control of his orchestra was unmatchable; like a skilled magician, he wielded his wand effectively. Though his hand gestures were light, like a butterfly's touch, sometimes barely visible, sometimes a bit flamboyant, more often gentle, it had the ability to convey a wide range of moods—soft, serene, calm, jubilant and grand—leaving the audience asking for more.

Mehta's 50-year-long association with the Israel Philharmonic Orchestra was guided by the music of his heart, the music of his soul, each time he appeared on stage. Mehta's posts as the Conductor Emeritus of the Los Angeles Philharmonic, and director for life of the Israel Philharmonic Orchestra, signify his musical genius.

Winner of the Padma Bhushan, the Padma Vibhushan, a recipient of the Kennedy Center Honors and several other honours, Mehta is an honorary citizen of Florence and Tel Aviv. Though he has retained his Indian citizenship, he is a permanent resident of the United States of America.

Mehta's mastery at controlling the tempo or tempi, the speed at which the music composition is played, was magical. In fact, Mehta's tempi was like his breathing; he could control it effortlessly and effectively, conveying a range of emotions through his music.

To conduct big orchestras like the Israel and the New York philharmonics with their brilliant musicians, each as gifted as the one sitting next to him or behind him, and to make a single voice emerge from these hundred talented soloists, isn't easy, but Mehta had the ability to subtly communicate to the orchestra as though it was a physical extension of himself. Mehta's sense of awe and wonder in his music was transmitted to both his orchestra and the audience.

Acknowledgements

My father, Motilal Chhabria, my forever guiding light, my superhero, watching and guiding me from the world beyond the clouds.

My mother, Sheela Chhabria, my cheerleader and my biggest critique.

My guru, Sadguru Mata Amritanandamayi Devi, my inspiration and strength.

Lord Ganesha for guiding my writing and blessing every stage of my writing.

My brother, Deepak Chhabria, for his suggestions and encouragement at every stage of this book.

Rudra Sharma, my amazing editor, for his patience and his complete belief in this book.

Upama Biswas and Manali Das for their meticulous editing and proofreading.

Sonia Madan for trusting me with this topic and starting the book's journey.

My family and close friends, who tolerated my seven-month-long absence that it took to research and write this book.